STRANGE

and

OBSCURE STORIES

of

WORLD WAR II

LITTLE-KNOWN TALES ABOUT THE
SECOND WORLD WAR

DON AINES

SKYHORSE PUBLISHING

Skyhorse Publishing books may be purchased in bulk at special discounts for sales promotion, corporate gifts, fund-raising, or educational purposes. Special editions can also be created to specifications. For details, contact the Special Sales Department, Skyhorse Publishing, 307 West 36th Street, 11th Floor, New York, NY 10018 or info@skyhorsepublishing.com.

Skyhorse® and Skyhorse Publishing® are registered trademarks of Skyhorse Publishing, Inc.®, a Delaware corporation.

Visit our website at www.skyhorsepublishing.com.

10 9 8 7 6 5 4 3 2

Library of Congress Cataloging-in-Publication Data is available on file.

Cover design by Mona Lin
Cover images: Getty Images
Interior images: Getty Images
Chapter icon: Getty Images, GeorgePeters, DigitalVision Vectors

Print ISBN: 978-1-5107-4685-5
Ebook ISBN: 978-1-5107-4686-2

Printed in the United States of America

Contents

Introduction

Ly father, two uncles, and an aunt were World War II
veterans. . . . Yeah, them and sixteen million other men
and women.

Dad, Don Sr., was born in 1926, the last birth year in which
men who reached draft age were able to go through basic and
advanced training and be deployed overseas for combat. He
fought in Germany during the last weeks of the war in Europe
and, thankfully, came through without a scratch. He was the
only one of the four to make the military a career, serving in
the Korean War and Vietnam War along the way. There were
other deployments: Japan in the weeks before North Korea
invaded South Korea, West Germany during the 1950s, and
Turkey in the 1960s. Then there were the assignments to stateside garden spots such as Fort Benjamin Harrison, Indiana;
Fort Riley, Kansas; Fort Gordon, Georgia; Fort Leavenworth,

Kansas; and the Pentagon. That's the short list. Army bases were not bad places for a kid to live, especially if your father was an officer. There was usually a parade ground with an artillery piece or two—I remember Fort Benjamin Harrison's parade ground had an M4 Sherman tank and a light tank, possibly an M3. We did not always live in base housing. The years in Washington were spent in an Ozzie and Harriet suburb, and all four of us sons got through the same high school because "The Colonel," as we boys called him, sandwiched two three-year Department of Defense assignments around his one year in Vietnam.

Dad liked "watching" baseball while lying on the couch with his eyes closed, and he liked watching westerns. He had no interest in war movies, although he found 1965's spot-the-star cinematic turkey "The Battle of the Bulge" laughable.

Uncle Phillip Aines was a bespectacled man with chiseled features, somewhat sturdier in build and slightly shorter than my six-foot, three-inch father. A serious student, he opted out of the Advanced Specialist Training Program, which kept some of the nation's best and brightest from seeing combat by enlisting them as privates while they took college courses. Phil was wounded serving with the U.S. Army's Tenth Division during the Ardennes offensive, probably by shrapnel from artillery or mortar fire. All we knew growing up was he had a bad leg, although he did not have a noticeable limp. I learned later he still had two legs because he won an argument with doctors who wanted to amputate the injured one. Phil went on to earn a PhD at Cornell, become a vice president of two major consumer-product corporations, and live a long life.

I know less about my maternal uncle, Jay Leon. He and Miriam, my mother's sister, settled in Phoenix sometime after the war. Miriam joined the Women's Army Corps during the war, and Jay was in the U.S. Army in the Pacific. Because they lived so far away from us, we didn't see Jay and Miriam all that many times, but Jay always struck me as a blunt-spoken bantamweight tough guy.

Those four veterans have passed from the scene, as have more than fifteen million other Americans who served during the war. The National WWII Museum estimates the number of survivors in 2020 at fewer than four hundred thousand. All would be in their nineties, with more than a few passing the century mark.

When I was a boy, none of these guys talked much about the war. Fortunately, my father set his experiences down on paper late in his life. His was not a strange or obscure story, just that of another serviceman doing his best to avoid being shot, shot down, incinerated, drowned, blown up, captured, or executed—same as most of the soldiers, sailors, airmen, and marines. They returned from the war to big cities and small towns, built the suburbs, and carried on with life. That goes also for the tens of millions of men and women from countries across the globe who served and fought in the war and the hundreds of millions of civilians who fell within its awful grasp.

Throughout this book will be quite a few references to films, not all of them flattering to Tinseltown. The reason is simple: Most people have seen a lot more World War II movies than they have read books on the war. Ninety minutes or two hours of sitting in a theater or watching television is easier than sitting down many more hours with a book. But if you are looking for a history lesson, Hollywood is not the place to find one.

There are a lot of numbers in the book, and some, even from reliable government sources, can vary depending on who did the counting. A staff sergeant with the Department of Defense POW/MIA Accounting Agency advised me that the official numbers for missing service personnel can vary from week-to-week. Some might also quibble with how many tons of explosives were packed into the bow of the *Campbeltown* when it rammed the drydock at St. Nazaire, or the top speed of a Hellcat, or the number of mules the army purchased in 1943, or how many soldiers served as extras in *Kolberg*. In most cases, numbers from official sources might not be exactly the same but fall within a reasonable margin.

Whenever practical, official military resources, museums, and historical sources are used. Books, magazine articles, movies, documentaries, websites, and videos were also mined to come up with these stories and are appropriately credited.

The culture-wide experience of the Second World War in America has only been matched a few other times in our history. The War of Independence, Civil War, and World War I also touched every city, town, village, and hamlet. Consider that those 16 million men and women in uniform represented about one person out of every eight of the 130 million Americans. The numbers of civilian males between eighteen and forty in towns and cities plummeted, with women and older workers filling huge gaps in the workforce. Today, about one out of every hundred Americans serve in the military out of a population of 330 million.

Each man and woman from the World War II era had a unique story. It belonged only to them.

Among those are some strange and obscure stories—more than enough to fill a few thousand books. Here are a few of them.

CHAPTER ONE
The Butcher's Bill

"One death is a tragedy. One million deaths a statistic."

—Unknown
(Often falsely attributed to Josef Stalin)

There's no record of Stalin having said that, or really anything like it. It's one of those too-good-to-be-true quotes that a magazine writer attributed to the dictator. Stalin might not have said those exact words, but the misquotation certainly sums up the character of a man responsible for so many millions of "statistics" and whose name became both a verb and adjective for rule by institutional terror and the cult of personality.

So, how many people died during World War II? The best estimates vary by millions from sixty-five million to one hundred million or more lives lost in the conflict, but there are several variables in any equation for figuring the butcher's bill for the war.

However, the question is fairly simple for the United States. The war began on December 7, 1941, and ended on September 2, 1945. During those 1,366 days the United States suffered 405,399 deaths, of which 291,557 occurred in or as a direct result of battle. The remaining deaths were a result of training and transport accidents, disease, and other causes not directly attributable to combat. The number also includes some 126 sailors who were killed when U-boats sank the destroyers USS *Kearny* and USS *Reuben James* in prewar battles in October 1941 when U.S. Navy vessels assisted convoys bound for Great Britain.

The U.S. Marines were in the middle of the bloodiest no-quarter battles of the war at Guadalcanal, Tarawa, Saipan, Peleliu, Iwo Jima, Okinawa, and scores of other islands in the Pacific. The corps lost 19,733 marines during the war, with 67,000 more wounded. The valor and sacrifice of the Marines has been duly and rightly celebrated in history books, novels, and especially Hollywood.

But the U.S. Army also fought in Asia, and in larger numbers. The army bore the brunt of the fighting in the Southwest Pacific theater in the Papua New Guinea campaign, the liberation of the Philippines, and scores of battles for beaches and islands that received little mention in the decades after the war. GIs were at Guadalcanal and Okinawa, but movies about those battles are often told from a marine perspective. Nevertheless, the war in the Pacific cost the army 57,137 lives.

For the Eighth Air Force, the skies over Europe proved bloodier than the sands of Iwo Jima and all the other marine battles of the Pacific. More than 26,000 airmen were killed in the war, and the Eighth Air Force's 47,483 total of dead and wounded represented about 40 percent of the 115,332 killed and wounded for all of the USAAF.

Excluding marine battle deaths, the U.S. Navy lost 34,607 sailors in all theaters, the Marines being deployed only in the Pacific. In the battle for Okinawa, the navy, its ships targeted by kamikaze attacks, lost 3,809 personnel, 912 more deaths than the Marines suffered in the island fighting.

The end date for counting casualties was December 31, 1946, presumably to account for those who died of lingering injuries, and for a fuller accounting of the missing. Included among the dead are the more than seventy-two thousand missing in action and presumed dead, a number that ebbs slowly downward as a few of the missing are recovered from one year to another, according to the Defense POW/MIA Accounting Agency.

To America's casualty list can be added 9,521 "civilian" deaths for the U.S. Merchant Marine, of which approximately half (4,780) went missing when their ships went down or they were blown overboard by an explosion or storm.

Along with the sixty-eight civilians killed at Pearl Harbor, hundreds more died or disappeared while interned or in the hands of the Germans and the Japanese. American civilians were killed in the Japanese invasions of the Philippines, Guam, and Wake Island—civilian contractors working on military construction jobs in the latter.

Among the American civilian deaths were those of a pregnant woman and five children on a church outing in Oregon on May 5, 1945. One member of the group happened upon a Fu-Go balloon bomb, one of thousands launched by the

Japanese. When the device went off, they became the only Americans killed in the continental United States during the war.

Compared to the countries that suffered the greatest slaughter—Russia, China, Germany, Poland, and Japan among them—it might seem the United States got off easy. Only in a statistical sense is that true. For any family, one death was still a tragedy, not a statistic.

For Great Britain and a few other nations, accurate accountings of the casualties were maintained, but they were in the minority among the combatants.

Europeans at least have some solid calendar dates to mark the beginning and end of hostilities: The Nazi invasion of Poland on September 1, 1939, prompted Britain and France to declare war two days later. But the Nazis had been engaged in relatively bloodless expansions in Austria and Czechoslovakia for a few years prior. The Soviets might have marked June 22, 1941, as the beginning of their war, as the Germans launched Operation Barbarossa. However, the Soviets were at war with Finland in 1939–40 and occupied the eastern half of Poland after the Germans attacked in the west.

The Red Army and the Japanese Imperial Army clashed for months during 1939 along the Manchuria-Mongolia border, culminating in the crushing defeat of the Japanese at the Battle of Khalkhin Gol. Though Japan later joined Germany and Italy to form the Axis, the Japanese never came to Germany's aid by again attacking the Soviets in the east. Historians can only speculate on how the course of the war might have changed had the Red Army been forced to fight on two fronts.

The beginning date of the war for China is even murkier. Japan occupied Manchuria following the Mukden Incident in 1931, but what was known as the Second Sino-Japanese War began July 7, 1937, when months of simmering tensions over Japan's increasing military presence in China erupted with the Marco Polo Bridge Incident.

For either China or the Soviets, casualties, both military and civilian, are impossible to calculate within a few million. Soviet military deaths range from the generally accepted (but amazingly specific) number of 8,668,400 to almost 11 million. The total deaths, including civilians who died of execution, starvation, exposure, disease, or collateral battle damage, raises the figure for total Soviet deaths to between 20 million and 27 million.

Accepting the high end of estimated Soviet deaths, about 13.7 percent of its population of 194 million were killed. That would mean one out of seven Soviets disappeared from the face of the earth. Abused by both the Nazis and Soviets during the war, Poland's population of thirty-five million was more than decimated—the loss of lives at about six million people represented 17 percent of its prewar population.

For the United States, the loss of life came to about one third of one percent. Each death was still a tragedy to the mothers, fathers, siblings, wives, sons, daughters, or sweethearts.

China, which was fighting a brutal civil war between the Nationalists and the Communists before, during, and after the war, estimated military losses of up to 3.7 million, while 8.2 million civilians were believed to have died as a result of military actions and Japanese war crimes. The highest estimate of deaths from the Rape of Nanking in 1937 is above two hundred thousand—again, a number difficult to pin down with any degree of accuracy. The estimate for deaths from war-related famine and disease fall within a huge range of between five to ten million.

In both the Soviet Union and China, the desperate circumstances engendered by enemy invasions made accurate head counts impractical. In both countries, civilians were taken from the streets and marched to the front when the exigencies of war demanded.

Some 5,533,000 German military personnel were killed during the war as they fought the Allies on multiple fronts—if one counts North Africa, the North Atlantic, and the Mediterranean along with Northwest Europe and the eastern front, according to the National WWII Museum. The number of civilian deaths range from 1.0 million to 2.5 million, less an estimate than an educated guess, it would seem. So many people in Europe and Asia were displaced by the war that accounting for all of them was impossible. Some had good reasons to not want to be found; many more went into captivity from which they never returned.

Add to these numbers the more than eleven million lives lost through the institutionalized murder in the Nazi death camps.

The tempo of civilian deaths accelerated in the closing months of the war as Allied armies pressed in from the eastern and western fronts, coupled with the deaths of hundreds of thousands incinerated, crushed, and blown to smithereens as British and American bombers, no longer harried by swarms of German fighters, pounded Berlin, Hamburg, Dresden, and other cities with impunity—and little accuracy. Death rained from the skies for the Japanese, as well, with American B-29

Superfortresses able to firebomb cities, while suffering acceptably low losses over those targets. The Superfortresses were each powered by four troublesome Wright R-3350 2,200-horsepower radial engines—one reason so much marine blood was shed to capture Iwo Jima for use as an emergency airfield for the bombers.

Despite fighting China on the continent and the United States across the Pacific, Japan's military deaths were estimated at 2.1 million, with another eight hundred thousand civilian deaths, mostly in the 1945 firebombings of its major cities and the atomic bombings of Hiroshima and Nagasaki. On the night of March 9–10, 1945, three hundred B-29 bombers flew in an X-pattern over Tokyo, dropping incendiary bombs and creating a firestorm, killing up to one hundred thousand people (almost exclusively civilians) and leaving one million more homeless. It was believed to be the deadliest night of the war, claiming more lives than Dresden, Hiroshima, or Nagasaki. Deaths from the Dresden raids of February 13–15, 1945, once estimated at 135,000, have been revised downward over the decades, with more recent estimates of around 25,000 fatalities.

"Killing Japanese didn't bother me very much at that time," said Major General Curtis E. LeMay, the man in charge of the B-29 bombing campaign. "It was getting the war over that bothered me."

Of the original Axis members, only the Italians had the sense to surrender when the Allies invaded Sicily, and they could see there was no hope of avoiding defeat. After years of failure after failure on the battlefield, the Grand Council of Fascism voted in July 1943 to give Mussolini the sack and return constitutional powers to the king. Unfortunately, the Nazis decided Italy had to be held and did so tenaciously against mostly American Fifth Army divisions forced to slog their way through the mud and mountains of the peninsula. Italy lost in excess of 320,000 of its soldiers and another 153,000 civilians.

Mussolini also sent about 250,000 soldiers to Russia to help out his pal Hitler. They fared no better against the Red Army and the Russian winter, with some 85,000 soldiers never to see their sunny homeland again.

While some countries listed their casualties by the hundreds of thousands and millions, most of the nations that sided with the Allies had little to do with the actual fighting. Much of Latin America from Mexico to Brazil entered the war on the side of the Allies. Military casualties were a few hundred for some countries and none for others, and civilian deaths were often the result of merchant shipping losses.

Switzerland was neutral during the war, but dozens of its citizens were killed when American bombers on several occasions wandered into Swiss airspace and unloaded on what the crews believed to be German targets. The Swiss gave almost as good as they got, knocking down several Allied bombers. More commonly, damaged American bombers would head for Switzerland, where the crews were interned for most of the war, rather than risk becoming prisoners of the Germans— or getting back to base to have another chance at earning a wooden cross.

Still a British colony during the war, India contributed 2.6 million troops to the Allied cause, fighting in North Africa, Burma, Italy, and other theaters. The Indians claimed the loss of eighty seven thousand soldiers during the war, predominantly in the China-Burma-India theater. However, estimates of civilian deaths range wildly from 1.5 million to 7.0 million. The majority of the civilian deaths were blamed on a 1943 famine in eastern India. The displacement of hundreds of thousands of ethnic Indians from Burma contributed to disruption of agriculture and food supplies in the northeast states, but other factors, such as drought or crop failure, are hard to pin specifically to the war. One Indian writer, Rakesh Krishnan Simha, makes the case that the British were perhaps more at fault than the Japanese, taking crops and transportation from the region in part to keep food, commodities, and equipment out of enemy hands in the event the Japanese invaded India, but also to supply its war effort in other parts of the globe. By the reckoning of many Indians, their deadliest enemy was not the Japanese, but their "ally" and overlord, Great Britain.

The final death toll for all countries lies somewhere between about 50 million and 100 million deaths. However many died, they were more than statistics on a sheet of paper.

CHAPTER TWO

A Triumph over War's Grim Reaper

"Our Frying Pans and Gridirons slay more than the Sword."

—John Adams in a letter to Abigail Adams,
April 13, 1777

Decades before Louis Pasteur's germ theory, the future president was on to one of the great truths of war: Filth, Disease, Malnutrition, and Mishap were the real Four Horsemen of the Apocalypse in war, much more so than spear and arrow, or musket and cannon in the millennia before the twentieth century.

World War II was the first of America's wars in which enemy action was the leading cause of death. The U.S. Department of Veterans Affairs lists 53,402 Americans killed in battle during this nation's nineteen months in World War I. The department lists 63,114 as having died of nonbattle causes. Disease came out ahead of the Germans in the Great War because of the Spanish flu pandemic of 1918, which killed upwards of one hundred million worldwide, nearly forty-seven thousand of whom were U.S. military personnel. The battle/nonbattle deaths flipped in the Second World War, with 291,557 killed as a result of combat against 113,842 noncombat deaths.

This trend continued into the Korean War, as noncombat deaths were less than 10 percent. In Vietnam, however, the number of nonbattle deaths rose to about one in five. (There were far more servicemen lost to noncombat causes outside the theater during the war. Those deaths are separate from Vietnam War casualties.) Nonbattle deaths again exceeded combat deaths 235 to 148 in Desert Shield/Desert Storm in 1990–91, as accidents proved more deadly than the Iraqi armed forces or disease. Life in the military is dangerous even in peacetime, as service members work regularly with large fuel- and explosives-laden equipment. The higher tempo of operations in wartime just increases the probability of accidental death.

What made the Germans and the Japanese more dangerous than accidents and disease was a combination of factors. Killing people became much more efficient on a day-to-day basis compared to World War I, when slaughters came in concentrated bursts at the Somme, Verdun, and other mindless frontal assaults against fixed fortifications. In the Second World War opposing forces could reach far beyond the frontlines, as mobile armored warfare was combined with tactical and strategic air attacks. For Germany, and to a lesser extent Britain, arms-production centers and civilian populations, transportation hubs, and sea lanes were vulnerable to attack. The war also lasted longer—several years longer depending on what date one uses to mark its outbreak.

World War II was also fought over a much greater area than the Great War, which was mostly limited to Europe and the Atlantic Ocean. The disruption of civilian populations far from the frontlines was widespread, resulting in the deaths of millions of noncombatants.

However, it was victory over infection and better medical care at the front that significantly cut into the death rate from disease and infection and saved countless limbs from amputation, especially for American and British servicemen. In World War II, guns beat germs on the scorecard of carnage.

Even today the name of Alexander Fleming likely pops up in high school biology classes for having discovered penicillin more or less by accident in 1928. It was not until the mid-1930s that Oxford University researchers Howard Walter Florey and Ernst Boris Chain developed a practical penicillin antibiotic. Florey took this knowledge to the United States, where researchers found a way to mass produce the antibiotic.

Fleming shared the 1945 Nobel Prize for Physiology and Medicine with Florey and Chain, the scientists who turned a mold into a practical and widely available life-saving drug. Fleming became a household name. Florey and Chain did not.

The work of scientists Ernst Chain and Howard Florey are unknown to most today. However, they helped save thousands of wounded from becoming fatalities during World War II. They might even have saved the person reading this page.

Another drug in wide use by medics and corpsmen during the war was sulfonamide, found in the 1930s—once again by the British—to be effective in the treatment of various infections and gonorrhea. This was a godsend to soldiers. One variant, M+B 693, was used to treat Winston Churchill for pneumonia in 1943. Before Christmas that year, he gave the manufacturer (M+B stood for the pharmaceutical firm May and Baker) as good a product endorsement as any company could hope for: "This admirable 'M+B,' from which I did not suffer any inconvenience, was used at the earliest moment and after a week's fever the intruders were repulsed."

Blood and plasma transfusions, better anesthetics, portable X-ray machines, and other technologies and techniques—plus better sanitation—saved thousands who would have otherwise joined the list of those who died of combat wounds.

It was no small matter that during the War of Independence the Prussian Baron von Steuben taught the Continentals to dig their latrines downstream of the source of their drinking water: it saved lives. Improvements in camp hygiene were also stressed by US Sanitary Commission in the Civil War. By the Second World War, the importance of camp cleanliness was military gospel.

By D-Day the Army Medical Corps had expanded to more than 132,000—up from less than 50,000 in 1939—and each division had a medical battalion. Sulfa powder poured into open wounds by army medics, the company aid squad and aid station (the collecting and clearing companies), and medical battalion headquarters all contributed to increased survival rates. Improved medical care extended all the way back to the United States, as the mortality rate among wounded soldiers was halved from eight in one hundred in the Great War to four in one hundred in World War II. Deaths from infection and disease were reduced by more than 90 percent.

More than six hundred U.S. soldiers came down with venereal diseases each day of the war, but, unlike World War I, antibiotics allowed almost all to return to duty.

Among the medics were many conscientious objectors, men who did not wish to take up arms on religious grounds but did not shirk military duty. The actor who played German soldier Paul Bäumer in *All Quiet on the Western Front* (1930) was one of them. After being classified a conscientious objector, Lew Ayres joined other "conchies" as a laborer at a CO camp in Wyeth, Oregon. In 1942 Ayres volunteered for the medical service and joined the army. Stateside, he rose to first-aid instructor with a rank of staff sergeant.

"He took a bust to pfc. [private first class] to become a chaplain's assistant" and go overseas, according to "Hollywood to New Guinea," an article that appeared in the July 21, 1944, edition of *Yank*. The author of the article caught up with a scrawny, mustachioed Ayres in an evacuation hospital on Wadke Island, New Guinea. The writer noted the actor's skin was yellowed by atabrine, the drug used to prevent malaria.

Actor Lew Ayres, left, took the horrors of war to heart while playing a World War I German soldier in *All Quiet on the Western Front* (1930). Nevertheless, the conscientious objector risked his life in the Pacific theater as a combat medic.

"I'm still a conscientious objector to war," Ayres said. "I want to continue this work, God willing. It's taken war to give me understanding of men and to find myself." He would find himself in combat in the Philippines a few months later.

Ayres did tell one whopper during the interview: "I never want to go back to pictures."

Combat medics went into battle without a weapon and with a big red-and-white Red Cross insignia on their helmets and brassards on their sleeves. Their noncombat status often was not respected, and that insignia served as a bull's-eye for enemy snipers. Some soldiers disdained the medics—until one crawled up to them under fire, stanched the bleeding of their sucking chest wound, and dragged them to safety.

Like a few million other GIs, my father went through what was referred to as a "short-arm inspection" by a bored medic (checking GI genitalia was likely a short-straw kind of assignment) to determine if he had picked up any sexually transmitted diseases after being on leave. He had not. Private Aines also had to undergo the frightening experience of combat dentistry, having developed a bad toothache in the Harz Mountains. His squad leader sent him to the company headquarters, which sent him on to the battalion aid station a mile or so behind the front lines. Back in 2004 he described the experience:

> The dentist (I don't know if he had a degree) sat me down in a collapsible chair. Beside it was a tripod with a foot treadle connected to a series of pulleys that drove the drill. Without administering a painkiller, the dentist began drilling. . . . At some point, the drill hung up in the tooth.

"Keep pedaling, damnit!" the dentist yelled at his assistant. He started drilling another tooth, but decided it wasn't worth the trouble. Giving me a local anesthetic, he pulled that tooth and another—only extractions rated pain medicine.

CHAPTER THREE

Hollywood Goes to War!

"Now for Australia and a crack at those Japs."

—Errol Flynn

The Tasmanian-born actor got to emote that wonderful line in *Desperate Journey*, perhaps the daffiest war movie released by Warner Bros., or any other studio, during the war.

Ready for the plot? Here goes: Flight Lt. Terrence Forbes (Flynn), American Flight Officer Johnny Hammond (Ronald Reagan), and the supporting cast take off on a supersecret mission over Germany. After a successful bombing run, they get shot down, and the survivors, including Arthur Kennedy and Alan Hale (the Skipper's father), are captured by the Nazis—but not for long. Reagan double-talks the Nazis into a state of confusion, and he and his fellow knights of the air overpower the guards and make good their escape. Before fleeing the Nazi compound, they find a map showing the location of a secret aircraft factory, which someone carelessly left on his desk. Needing to get the map back to England, they hop a train and find themselves in Hermann Goering's private railcar! While the train takes them in comfort into Berlin, they take time to sabotage a chemical plant en route. (This is a good time to catch your breath.)

Once in Berlin, the guys luckily bump into members of the anti-Nazi German underground. But the Nazis find their lair, and in the ensuing shootout Alan Hale doesn't make it. However, our boys are still one step ahead of the martinet Nazi officer in his comic opera uniform (Canadian Raymond Massey), and the stooges who "ja voll" his every order. Now reduced in number, the survivors come upon a captured British bomber, fueled up and loaded to wreak some havoc over England. Forbes, Hammond, and Flying Officer Jed Forrest (Kennedy's character) steal the plane, using its machine guns to mow down a few dozen of those lousy krauts as they taxi down the runway. While flying back to England, the guys decide to bomb one more Nazi target, and Flynn delivers that rousing last line.

Despite a plot better suited to other Warner Bros. stars—Bugs Bunny, Daffy Duck, and Porky Pig—this film went on to pull in nearly $4 million, a tidy sum back in the day.

Flynn got his crack at the Japs three years later in 1945's *Objective, Burma!*, leading a platoon-sized unit of American paratroopers who jump behind enemy lines on a mission to destroy a Japanese radar station in the middle of the jungle.

This is a far less jocular film than *Desperate Journey*. The United States was just getting into the war when the former was filmed. By 1945 the war was nearing its bloody crescendo, the United States had suffered hundreds of thousands of deaths, and the movie took a more somber approach to its story.

The film still has a few hoots. Flynn's character, Capt. Nelson, jumps from a C-47 holding his carbine in one hand, a sure way to enter combat unarmed. It strains credulity to have character actor George Tobias pretending to be a paratrooper, as he was in his mid-forties and it was hard to tell exactly where his waistline was located. Harder to figure was the casting of Henry Hull as war correspondent Mark Williams. Hull turned fifty-five that year and didn't look a day over seventy. The box office for this film was also about $4 million. At the time of its release, *Objective, Burma!* drew the scorn of some British, who felt it made an American show out of a British theater.

The China-Burma-India theater was primarily a British and Commonwealth show, but the United States played a major supporting role and had a unit that took part in long-range patrols behind Japanese lines: Merrill's Marauders. Their story was one of incredible sacrifice, privation, and violence, where the jungle was almost as great an enemy as the Japanese. Jeff Chandler portrayed Frank Merrill in the 1962 film, *Merrill's Marauders*.

Destination Tokyo (1943) starred Cary Grant as the commander of the USS *Copperfin*, a submarine crewed by saintly sailors on a mission to gather meteorological and intelligence data prior to the Doolittle Raid in 1942. The sailors are the usual cross-section of white American ethnic groups and stock characters—Alan Hale shows up as the cook, dispensing comic relief and middle-aged wisdom. John Garfield gets most of the sanitized wisecracks in this Warner Brothers offering.

One bit of risqué phallic humor was either overlooked or given a wink and a nod by censors. Written on the side of a torpedo being inserted into the firing tube were "Open wide Tojo" and "Try this on for size." Maybe the Hays Office just didn't get the joke.

What these films lacked in verisimilitude they made up for in being highly, sometimes wildly, entertaining, if the viewer checked his or her sense of reality at the ticket counter. Even now on Turner Classic Movies they are a fast-paced and fun way to waste two hours. Given the strictures of the Production Code that existed at the time, and the desire by the studios to promote stateside morale, films like *Desperate Journey*, *Objective, Burma!*, and *Operational Pacific* were not bad—not bad at all.

But if you are looking for a history lesson, you won't find one in a movie theater. *Mission to Moscow*, also perpetrated by Warner Bros., was the filmization of the book by Joseph E. Davies, the first United States ambassador to the Soviet Union. ONE AMERICAN'S JOURNEY INTO THE TRUTH! screams the poster. One of a few films during the war to promote goodwill toward the USSR, which, after all, did the bulk of the fighting and dying in Europe, the movie portrays the Moscow show trials not as a purge of Stalin's real and imagined enemies but as a search for Nazi fifth columnists. A scene in a Moscow department store makes the USSR seem more a shoppers' paradise than workers' paradise. "Uncle Joe" Stalin makes a cameo as played by Manart Kippen, a somewhat less threatening presence than the real deal.

MGM's big-budget *Dragon Seed* should rank high on any list of well-meaning propaganda misfires. Katharine Hepburn and Walter Huston lead a largely Caucasian cast in the Pearl S. Buck story about the lives of Chinese villagers under occupation of the Japanese Imperial Army. Going by the IMDb cast list, one must read down thirteen names before coming across an Asian actor: Clarence Lung, a native of Boise, Idaho. This does not count Turhan Bey who, although half Turkish, was born in Vienna, Austria. In some scenes Hepburn looks as uncomfortable as her makeup must have felt, and the script has its share of Charlie Chan pseudo-Chinese dialogue.

Not every U.S. or Allied war film was as full of timeworn clichés, comic-book heroics, and central-casting characters as the examples cited above. MGM's *Thirty Seconds over Tokyo*, (1944) with Spencer Tracy and Van Johnson, had reasonably natural acting for the period, great flying scenes, and Oscar-winning special effects. Robert Walker is a bit too "gee whiz, fellas," and one character has a southern accent and accompanying Dixie patter that would sound better coming out of Foghorn Leghorn's beak. Robert Mitchum and most of the supporting cast avoid such caricatures.

The British produced films of some quality and originality during the war, despite the privations wartime shortages imposed on its citizens. Those shortages, particularly of food, made some scenes in the otherwise nuanced *The Spy in Black* seem just wrong. Conrad Veidt as the not-so-awful Nazi spy enters the cottage of double agent Valerie Hobson and looks aghast upon a brick-sized block of butter, the message being the Germans were starving while the Scots at least were enjoying a bounty. In another scene, a character slices into a huge ham. Both scenes must have drawn rueful chortles from British audiences, losing weight on their not-quite-starvation war-ration diets. Michael Powell directed and Emeric Pressburger coscripted in their first of several collaborations, usually as codirectors.

Real-life British Army officer David Niven took time off from actual warfare to film *The Way Ahead*, directed by Carol Reed and released in 1944. The story follows a group of recruits from basic training to North Africa, with Niven as a very professional but humane platoon leader. He is aided by a very fine supporting cast: Stanley Holloway (*My Fair Lady*), Trevor Howard (*Brief Encounter*), and other actors better recognized in America by face than name. A very young Peter Ustinov acted in and coscripted the film with Eric Ambler. The Tommies in the film probably came across as stock characters and stereotypes to British audiences but seem to have more dimension than the GIs in American movies.

Niven wrote many a wonderful story about his early years in England and Hollywood in *The Moon's a Balloon* and *Bring on the Empty Horses* but said little about his experience in the war. Niven had this to say about his war experience:

> I was asked by some American friends to search out the grave of their son at Bastogne. I found it where they told me I would, but it was among 27,000 others, and I told myself that here, Niven, were 27,000 reasons why you should keep your mouth shut after the war.

Powell, Pressburger, and Niven collaborated in 1946's *Stairway to Heaven*, which can only be described as a fantasy war romance. Niven, as Squadron Leader Peter Carter, somehow survives what was supposed to have been a fatal fall from a burning bomber into the English Channel. Instead, he washes up alive on a Devon beach and falls in love with Kim Hunter. His survival complicates the afterlife of the foppish French angel (Marius Goring) who botched the job of escorting Carter to the "other world." The film jumps back and forth from the Technicolor real world to the washed-out hues of the other world. In the former, Carter is diagnosed with a brain tumor and operated on. In the latter, a judge and jury of soldiers, sailors, and airmen from wars past and present must reach a verdict as to whether Carter will be granted a second chance at life. There is a huge escalator to the other world in *Stairway to Heaven*, which was released in the United States under the title *A Matter of Life and Death*. By either title, it is a beautiful and original film.

British playwright Noël Coward's contribution to the war effort was 1942's *In Which We Serve*, codirected with the great David Lean (*Bridge on the River Kwai* and *Lawrence of Arabia*). Coward plays Capt. E. V. Kinross, whose destroyer HMS *Torrin* survives many battles before succumbing to enemy bombers off Crete. The adventures of ship and crew are told mostly in flashback as the sailors struggle to survive in the Mediterranean. The story sort of mirrors that of HMS *Kelly*, which also met its end in the Mediterranean under the command of Lord Mountbatten. For one of the few times in his career, Coward steps away from his tuxedo and cigarette-holder image, ably assisted by John Mills, Michael Wilding, Celia Johnson, and a host of other familiar Brit faces.

Desperate Journey and *Objective: Burma!* are bookends to the portrayal of the war by Hollywood during the fighting, but filmmakers in both the United States and Britain were setting the popular-culture table before the opening shots were fired. *Sergeant York* with Gary Cooper (1941) reminded American viewers of the war against the Kaiser and our nation's greatest hero of the conflict. A year earlier, Joel McCrea played a newspaper reporter following the trail of agents from a never-named European power in Alfred Hitchcock's *Foreign Correspondent*. Germany and Hitler are never mentioned by name, even though the war was already underway by the time of its release and the British certainly knew who wore the black hats.

Just months before the Nazis invaded Poland, Warner Bros. released *Confessions of a Nazi Spy* with Edward G. Robinson as the government agent out to bust the ring. The movie had no problem calling out the bad guys by name.

Fire over England (1937), a costume drama about thwarting the Spanish Armada, can be viewed as an early morale booster for the Brits, many of whom could already see the storm clouds gathering on the continent. It was also the first screen pairing of Laurence Olivier and Vivien Leigh. Two years later and just two months before the Germans invaded Poland, Sir Larry was doing battle with thinly disguised German spies out to steal British military aircraft technology in *Q Planes*, which was later retitled *Clouds over Europe*, possibly to make a connection with the earlier (and better) film. Laurence pilots one of the aircraft, which is brought down by a mysterious ray fired from a mysterious ship, the *Viking*. Although the enemy is never named, everyone onboard the ship speaks in a suspiciously Germanic accent and the film was released only six months before the real war started.

Two years before *Foreign Correspondent*, Hitchcock, at that time still working in England, directed *The Lady Vanishes* in which Dame May Whitty plays the unlikely English agent kidnapped by spies from an, again, unnamed European power. The bad guys once again speak in suspiciously Germanic accents.

In 1940 Columbia Pictures produced *You Nazty Spy!*, featuring three of its most popular thespians, Moe, Larry, and Curly. Moe's portrayal of Moe Hailstone, figurehead dictator of Moronica, preceded Charlie Chaplin's *The Great Dictator* by a few months.

Chaplin plays the dual roles of Jewish ghetto barber and Adenoid Hynkel, dictator of Tomania. Take a guess who he is supposed to be. The film hits its stride when Hynkel holds summit with Benzino Napaloni, the supremo of Bacteria. The movie has some great comedy bits but ends on an odd note with the barber, now masquerading as Hynkel, addressing a Nuremberg-size crowd with one of those "brotherhood of man, workers unite" speeches.

In the immediate aftermath of the war, the tone of films changed. *The Best Years of Our Lives* earned the Best Picture Oscar of 1946 for its portrayal of a trio of veterans returning to their midwestern hometown. The Oscar for Best Supporting Actor went to Harold Russell, a nonactor who lost both hands in an explosion during a training exercise at a stateside army camp.

The readjustment of soldiers, sailors, and marines to civilian life after the war became the grist for a host of movies such as *Till the End of Time*, *Crossfire*, *The Men*, and *Bright Victory*, to name a handful.

Between 1942 and 1945 Hollywood devoted much of its energies to war-related films, but still cranked out musicals, comedies, westerns, and mysteries. Oddly, only two war-themed films won Best Picture Oscars during that period: *Mrs. Miniver* and *Casablanca*. The GIs overseas lucky enough to see a movie now and then likely wanted to see a Bugs Bunny cartoon followed by Esther Williams in *Bathing Beauty*, over the Tinseltown heroics of *The Purple Heart* or *The Fighting Seabees*. Those two films were standouts in portraying the Japanese, then called by the slur "Japs," as buck-toothed, sneering savages wearing Coke-bottle glasses. Especially cringeworthy is the samurai victory dance in *The Purple Heart*.

Of course, Hollywood in a few cases added a healthy helping of cheese to its World War II films. Part of the promotion for *The Seventh Cross*, a dead serious 1944 Spencer Tracy vehicle about George Heisler, a political prisoner trying to escape the gestapo, had a Tracy look-alike, Roy Thomas, roaming the country with prizes of $500 war bonds offered for those who spotted the "fugitive."

During the war, Hollywood could not portray the horror of battle with any degree of reality. The Production Code limited the amounts and types of gore that could be portrayed in film. When American actors died in "battle" it was heroically—a short speech before going limp in the arms of a comrade—or anonymously, like the extras being gunned down behind John

Wayne. The studios, and the government, had to consider the impact of such entertainments on public morale.

Even documentaries were scrubbed or padded with staged scenes. The Army initially resisted the release of John Huston's documentary *The Battle of San Pietro* about a 1943 U.S. Army assault on an Italian village because it might negatively affect military and civilian morale. Though it contains its share of staged footage, there was nothing staged about the images of dead Americans being placed in white body bags. The half-hour film was finally released a few days before Germany's surrender.

Most movie stars whose names people can still remember to this day remained civilians during the war, but some put on real uniforms—James Stewart and Clark Gable in the U.S. Army Air Force being the best-known among them. Here are a few others:

- Tyrone Power starred in period pieces and costume epics, often forced to wear foppish outfits in his prewar films. Already a trained pilot, he joined the marines and flew cargo in, and wounded out, of Iwo Jima and Okinawa.
- Robert Montgomery starred in *Night Must Fall* and *Here Comes Mr. Jordan* before the war. The credits in the PT Boat film *They Were Expendable* (1945) listed him as Lieutenant Commander Robert Montgomery. He really did serve in PT boats and destroyers during the war.
- Douglas Fairbanks Jr. lent his easy charm to *The Prisoner of Zenda* and *The Corsican Brothers* before the war. During it, he had a distinguished career in the U.S. Navy, seeing

action in the Mediterranean and promoting the creation of a naval deception unit known as the Beach Jumpers to draw enemy forces away from actual landing sites.

- Tim Holt gave an interesting performance in Orson Welles's *The Magnificent Ambersons* (1942) before joining the USAAF. A B-29 bombardier, he was wounded in a raid over Japan on the war's last day. He came home to star alongside Humphrey Bogart and Walter Huston in *The Treasure of the Sierra Madre* in 1948, before settling into a comfortable career in B westerns.

- Audie Murphy was turned down by the marines, so the Texas killing machine joined the army. The most decorated U.S. soldier of the war went on to have a pretty good career before his untimely death in the 1971 crash of a private airplane in Virginia.

Many other soldiers, sailors, marines, and airmen ended their service as anonymous as when they went in but gained celebrity when they took up playacting:

- Mel Brooks, who directed and/or acted in *The Producers*, *Blazing Saddles*, and *Young Frankenstein*, was a combat engineer with the army, clearing land mines in Europe.

- Don Adams was Maxwell Smart, Secret Agent 86, on *Get Smart*, cocreated by fellow veteran Mel Brooks. "Would you believe . . ." Adams served with the marines at Guadalcanal and later as a drill instructor?

- Bernice Frankel might have better fit the image of a tough-talking marine sergeant than Adams. Under her professional name, Beatrice Arthur, she gained fame as the acid-tongued matron in the television sitcom *Maude*.

- On his forty-fourth mission as a B-25 bombardier, Russell Johnson was shot down while bombing a Japanese base in the Philippines. Johnson broke both ankles when his plane ditched. Two decades later he was involved in a boating accident, and the "professor" was stranded on *Gilligan's Island* for three seasons.

- Marine scout sniper Lee Marvin's luck ran short on his twenty-first island assault. On Saipan, a Japanese machine-gun bullet severed his sciatic nerve and left him hospitalized for thirteen months. This real tough guy had some cred when he played heavies in *The Wild One* and *Bad Day at Black Rock*, or hard-edged heroes in *Point Blank* and *The Dirty Dozen*.

CHAPTER FOUR

The Greatest Escapes

*"Suddenly it hit me. You're the dumbest pilot that ever
flew a plane."*

—Bob Hoover

A s he went wheels up at the end of an enemy airstrip, Bob
Hoover had plenty of reasons to question whether what
he had done was a smart move. Shot down in February 1944
over the Mediterranean Sea south of France and fished out of
the frigid waters by a German patrol boat, he had spent more
than a year imprisoned at Luft Stalag I near Barth, Germany.

Now, he was in the cockpit of a Focke-Wulf 190 single-seat
fighter, the same type of aircraft that sent him into the drink
a year before. He was stealing it from a lightly guarded aerodrome where dozens of Luftwaffe aircraft in various states of
disrepair littered the field. It also crossed Hoover's mind that

the war in Europe was weeks, if not days from a complete Allied victory, and he might have been reasonably safe had he just cooled his heels until a Russian tank came bursting through the gates to liberate the stalag's thousands of POWs. Eisenhower had even put out the word for Allied prisoners to sit tight.

"I should have sat there like everyone else, but it was in my mind . . . to never give up," Hoover said in a video interview decades later. Besides, most of the guards knew the end was near, and many were not taking their jobs too seriously.

It also occurred to the fighter-stealing pilot that he was behind the stick of a plane of questionable airworthiness with Luftwaffe markings at a time when Allied air superiority was complete. American and British fighter pilots roaming the skies would have likely jumped the FW to add a kill to their record were they to spot him.

Hoover and a fellow POW escaped Luft Stalag I while guards dealt with a staged fight involving hundreds of prisoners. Hoover remarked in one interview that, with the end of the Third Reich fast approaching, some guards had become lax in their duties. That might have been so, but guards were a mixed lot: wounded soldiers unfit for frontline duty, those who were too old to serve, and often those too mentally unbalanced or of such low mentality that they could not be trusted for regular military service. Then, too, some guards undoubtedly had family and friends killed at the fronts or by the carpet-bombing and firebombing of Hamburg, Dresden, Berlin, or other targeted cities.

Hoover and the other escapee wandered the countryside, coming to a farmhouse where a *hausfrau* graciously fed her erstwhile enemies. "She gave us eggs, which we hadn't had in more than a year," Hoover recalled. Further along, they encountered another woman emerging from a house waving a handgun.

"This will do you more good than it will me," the woman said in broken English. Hoover and his companion commandeered a pair of bicycles and pedaled through enemy territory until they came upon the airfield, littered with damaged and cannibalized aircraft. They encountered a mechanic who, confronted by the armed escapees, decided his life was not worth sacrificing for his crumbling fatherland.

"We found this one, it had a lot of damage, but it was full of fuel," Hoover remembered. His fellow POW declined risking a ride in the single-seater, preferring to take his chances on foot, or bicycle. The man survived the war, and Hoover would meet up with him years later.

"I had no parachute and I was in an enemy airplane . . . I could hardly see out because I didn't have a seat cushion or a parachute," said Hoover. Peering over the control panel and through the canopy windscreen, he gunned the engine and pulled out of the revetment, not even bothering to taxi onto the runway, but heading across a grass field to get airborne.

"I didn't know where I was going, except I had a compass," Hoover said in a 2014 interview.

Bob Hoover took off to risk the kind of escape only a character played by Errol Flynn or James Garner would pretend to tackle. The future test pilot pointed the FW's prop to the west in search of windmills.

****

Millions of combatants fell into enemy hands during the war: Poles, gathered in by the Germans and Soviets, in 1939; tens of thousands of French poilus and British Tommies as France collapsed in the spring of 1940; entire armies of Red Army soldiers in the months after Hitler launched Operation Barbarossa in June 1941; tens of thousands more Brits and thousands of Yanks when the Philippines, Malaysia, Singapore, and Hong Kong fell to the Japanese Imperial Army onslaught in 1941–42.

In 1942 and early 1943, the momentum switched permanently as the U.S. Navy sank four Japanese Imperial Navy aircraft carriers at Midway, the British put the Afrika Korps back on its heels at El Alamein, and the Soviets won the battle of attrition at Stalingrad. From that point on, it was predominantly the Allies bagging Axis soldiers in huge numbers, although few Japanese would lay down their arms in the no-quarter battles of the Pacific theater. True to their *Bushido* code, Japanese soldiers chose death over dishonor, preferring to end their lost causes, on Tarawa, Iwo Jima, Okinawa, and a few hundred forgotten island and jungle battles, with a *banzai* charge. Capture was almost an accident for the Japanese warrior.

British and Commonwealth forces bagged tens of thousands of poorly led, badly equipped, and badly trained Italian troops in North Africa before Irwin Rommel and the Afrika Korps turned the tables and did the same to the Allies at Tobruk and other victories. But 175,000 Germans surrendered when cornered in Tunisia at the end of the North African campaign.

Captured Italian soldiers adapted well to life in U.S. prisoner of war camps, where they were generally treated humanely and fed well, although in one camp they staged a strike over the poor quality of their olive oil ration. Many contributed to the Allied war effort—Italian POWs provided much of the labor for construction of warehouses and other buildings at Letterkenny Army Depot near Chambersburg, Pennsylvania, including the depot's chapel.

Germans proved another matter. *Soldaten* swore an oath of allegiance to Hitler, and many nurtured that loyalty and fanaticism behind the barbed wire of American camps, particularly those captured early in the war. More than two thousand of the more than two hundred thousand held in the United States made escape attempts but were hunted down in quick order. Getting out of a camp in Arizona or Oregon was one thing. Getting across a continent, across an ocean, through Allied lines, and back to Germany was an impossibility.

The end of the war did not mean quick repatriation for thousands of other Axis prisoners held in the United States or Great Britain. Instead, they continued in forced labor in Western Europe, some not allowed to return to their home countries until 1948.

The Soviets kept hundreds of thousands of Axis prisoners long after the war, releasing the last of those they admitted having in 1955. Most never returned, either dying in captivity or otherwise disappearing in the gulags, never to be heard from again.

The odds of survival were best for British, Commonwealth, and American prisoners in the hands of the Germans, with a mortality rate of between 1 and 4 percent during captivity. The disparity in that estimate is due in part to the forced relocation of Allied prisoners in the closing months of the war as the

Allies closed in on Germany. Thousands of POWs were moved by march or rail to new camps during the winter and early spring of 1945. Exposure, pneumonia, starvation, and execution resulted in the deaths of unknown numbers of prisoners.

The death rate among Western Allies held by the Japanese was nearly 40 percent, as the Japanese, who were not signatories to the Geneva Convention, held those who surrendered in low regard, working many to death building a railway through Burma or in mines and factories on the home islands. Of the 27,465 U.S. service members who surrendered to or were captured by the Japanese, 11,107 died. Those captured during the island campaigns were often just tortured and killed. Unfortunately, many Allied prisoners also died when U.S. submarines and aircraft attacked and sank unmarked Japanese prison ships.

Most Allied prisoners of war languished in camps until liberated by advancing friendly forces, or by the release of death through forced labor, starvation, exposure, disease, and extermination. The odds of a successful escape were long.

The March 1944 escape from Luft Stalag III, the subject of a best-selling nonfiction book and the highly fictionalized Hollywood movie *The Great Escape*, is a case in point. James Garner and Donald Pleasance did not steal an airplane, and Steve McQueen did not jump a barbed-wire fence on a motorcycle, but one fact the film got right was the body count: of the seventy-six men who made it out of the tunnel, just three escaped to freedom, twenty-three were recaptured, and fifty were executed. Unlike the film, where most of the doomed POWs are machine-gunned in a mountain meadow, the Germans instead shot them by the ones and twos as they were caught. If the point was to be "a thorn in the side" of the Germans, the "great escape" did not draw any divisions off the eastern front. Most of the dirty work was done by police, gestapo, and home guard soldiers.

Other mass escapes fared worse:

- Prisoners at the Sobibor extermination camp in Poland engineered a breakout on October 14, 1943, killing several guards, taking their weapons, and rushing the gates. More than 150 died in the attempt, either from gunfire or land mines sewn in fields bordering the camp. Over a hundred more were hunted down and killed by pursuing soldiers and police. Fewer than sixty were known to have survived the war. The long odds of escape, however, were better than waiting for the Russians: the United States Holocaust Memorial Museum estimates that upwards of two hundred thousand Jews and other prisoners were murdered at Sobibor.

- Japanese POWs at a camp near Cowra, Australia, organized a breakout on August 5, 1944, gang-rushing the guards. More than half of the eleven hundred Japanese prisoners escaped into the countryside. All 545 escapees were accounted for within days, either recaptured, killed, or dead by their own hands. The death toll was 235.

- For prisoners held by the gestapo and doomed to execution at a compound in Amiens, France, their chance at freedom came like a bolt out of the blue on February 18, 1944. Acting on intelligence from the French Resistance, eighteen RAF Mosquitos roared in just feet above the surrounding snow-covered fields, skipping their bombs into the jail's wall. About one hundred prisoners were killed in the bombing, along with many of their captors, but more than two hundred condemned prisoners ran through the breached wall, some to awaiting Resistance fighters who staged getaway vehicles in the vicinity. Alas, many were recaptured and doubtless met the fate that awaited them at Amiens, but a slim chance is better than none.

What makes a prisoner want to escape, beyond the universal instinct to be physically unfettered and free of the threat of arbitrary execution or slow death by starvation or disease? Who would burrow hundreds of feet with spoons and tin cups in unimaginably claustrophobic conditions, or cut through concertina wire and crawl through minefields, only to risk being hunted down and summarily shot?

For the Western Allies, many POWs were from RAF Bomber Command and RAF Fighter Command, and were Americans from the Eighth Army Air Force. Through the winnowing process, the air forces of America and the United Kingdom selected their very best to pilot and crew fleets of bombers and fighter aircraft. These officers and NCOs were among the best-trained, most intelligent, most aggressive, and most physically fit men the Allied nations had to offer. Pilots, navigators, and flight engineers were among the captured, though these survivors accounted for about one in five of those shot down over enemy territory. Max Hastings, author of *Bomber Command*, put the cost in lives of Britain's bomber crews at 55,573, with another 9,784 taken prisoner. "The Mighty Eighth," which did not get into the thick of the strategic bombing campaign until late 1942, lost over 26,000 crewmen. For all the USAAF units

serving in the European and Mediterranean theaters of operation, about 30,000 were killed and 33,000 spent the war as
"kriegies," short for the German tongue-twisting term for prisoners of war, *Kriegsgefangener* These men faced constant gnaw-
ing hunger, boredom, cold during winter, back-breaking labor,
lice, diseases, poor medical care, often sadistic guards, and the
knowledge that their lives and futures were in the hands of an
enemy who might be ordered to execute them should the war
become a lost cause. One way for POWs to take a measure of
control over their fates was to plan an escape. The chances of a
"home run" back to friendly forces were slim to none, and few
prisoners were willing to take those odds.

In Homer's *The Iliad,* Ulysses used the deception of
a wooden horse to gain entry to and defeat Troy. In 1943,
three British officers, with the aid of many other POWs, used
another wooden horse to get out of Luft Stalag III, months
before the more well-known Great Escape.

The brilliance of the plan was in its simplicity. Why
dig a long tunnel underneath a barracks to the barbed-wire
fences and to the surrounding woods when the exercise yard
was much closer to the goal line? The Nazis expected escape
attempts, but the likely places to begin digging a tunnel were
under the barracks, showers, latrines, or other structure over
which the prisoners had a level of privacy and control. Those
structures were also set well back from the fences. The guards
would not expect to catch prisoners shoveling a hole in the
middle of an exercise yard. Yet that is exactly what Lt. Michael
Codner, Flight Lt. Eric Williams, and Canadian Flight Lt.
Oliver Philpot did, while cleverly masking their work. That's
where the pommel horse came in. Each day the prisoners

carried the wooden horse, made from wood left over from Red Cross packages, out to the yard and endlessly practiced their vaulting skills. Later they would carry the horse back to the barracks and, the next day, repeat the exercise. Concealed inside the horse was Codner or Williams. Out in the yard, one of them would begin digging for the day, scooping out dirt and placing it in sacks hung inside the horse. At the end of a session, the prisoner would place a wooden cover for the hole a few inches below grade, hiding it with a layer of dirt. His comrades would then carry the horse and the digger back to the barracks.

The Germans were not total stooges: the pommel horse raised their suspicions, and it was thoroughly inspected. Digging did not begin immediately, and a prisoner would occasionally (and intentionally) knock the horse over to demonstrate to the guards that nothing was going on underneath. Williams and Codner then got to their task of excavating the tunnel, while Philpot handled the logistics of getting the men to carry out the horse, do the endless vaulting and later dispose of each day's diggings. That was no simple task, as the soil from a few feet below ground was a yellowish sand. It has to be hidden, mixed into the soil of the prisoner garden or spread about and inconspicuously mixed with the topsoil of the yard.

It is almost incomprehensible what level of hunger and boredom—combined with dogged determination and ingenuity—would drive men to set aside their fears of being buried alive in a tunnel collapse just for the faint chance of somehow making it back to England. The tunnel was less than three feet high and wide, perhaps dimensions of an American telephone booth laid on its side. Darkness was relieved only by candles, and the air grew stale and unhealthy as the tunneler exhaled more and more carbon dioxide into the confined space. Codner survived a cave-in that nearly exposed the plot, as a small hole opened up at the surface. A quick-thinking POW feigned an injury and lay down over the hole while Codner managed to shore up the collapsed section. In the latter stages of burrowing, as the prisoners got farther and farther away from the entrance that provided what little fresh air got to them, a pipe was used to poke air holes through to the surface a few feet above.

A few years after the war ended, British filmmakers chronicled one of the few successful "home run" escapes from a German stalag in *The Wooden Horse*.

This went on for three months until the tunnel was completed on October 29, 1943, and the trio made their break disguised as French laborers. This required more sleight of hand by Codner, Williams, and Philpot, who could not simply dig up the tunnel entrance and jump in. Once the horse was used to get them into the tunnel, another prisoner was hidden inside to recover the entrance one last time.

Codner and Williams went off together while Philpot struck out alone. Smuggled aboard a merchantman, Williams and Codner hid in the bilge on the voyage from Stettin in Germany to Copenhagen in Denmark. From there they were taken by fishing boat to neutral Sweden. Philpot was there days earlier, having gotten to Danzig and then by ship to Sweden. The three contacted British authorities in the neutral Scandinavian country and were flown back to England.

Williams wrote *The Wooden Horse* after the war. In 1950 British Lion Film Corporation released an excellent film on the escape, although for some reason the names of the real-life escapees were changed.

****

Bob Hoover was sweating out his escape to friendly lines, hoping the damaged FW 190 would stay aloft. He flew it low, taking advantage of cloud cover to avoid being bounced by British or American fighters.

At last "the windmills were coming up in Holland, and they hated the Germans," Hoover said in the interview two years before his death in 2016 at the age of 94. He put the FW down in a plowed field, but his welcoming committee was an angry group of farmers armed with pitchforks.

"They were Dutchmen, thinking I was a German," he told the interviewer. Hoover put his hands up and tried to explain why an American was flying a German warplane. Luckily, a

British Army truck came along, and a soldier told them the incredible story.

"I say, old chap, hop in," one of the Tommies told Hoover.

It was a story Hoover would tell over and over in the next seven decades. It would be enough to get free drinks or meals for the rest of his life, but Hoover had many more adventures throughout his legendary flying career.

Two-and-a-half years after his escape, Hoover just missed becoming a household name. Instead it was Chuck Yeager who took the controls of the Bell X-1 rocket plane on October 14, 1947, breaking the sound barrier.

"Richard Frost, Bell project engineer, was flying low chase that morning, and Lt. Bob Hoover was flying high chase well ahead of the B-29, both in Lockheed P-80s," Yeager later recalled. "I lighted the first chamber, aiming for Hoover's P-80 about ten miles ahead."

Yeager in sequence lit the four liquid-fuel rocket motors, pointed the needle nose of the orange X-1 toward the heavens, and zoomed past his wingman and into the history books.

Beside being war veterans and test pilots, Hoover and Yeager also shared the experience of being shot down by German Folke-Wulfe 190s over France. Yeager was on his eighth mission when his P-51 Mustang was jumped by three 190s near Bordeaux on March 4, 1944. Instead of his parachute drifting him down into a German patrol, the 21-year-old found himself surrounded by members of the French Resistance. They smuggled Yeager to the border of neutral Spain, and, from there, he made it to Gibraltar. His evasion from capture came with some close calls: Yeager escaped when a German patrol opened fire on him and a companion, with the other man having a leg blown off. The British got Yeager back to England, and he got back into a cockpit, becoming an ace with thirteen kills by war's end, with five shoot-downs coming on a single mission.

****

The war effort absorbed a huge proportion of American males between the ages of eighteen to forty-five to feed the man-power needs of the military; despite the supposed patriotic fervor of the times, two-thirds of them were drafted. Still, the services rejected about a third of those it called in, the Great Depression having left many men unfit for duty, leaving them undernourished, underweight, nearly toothless, and debil-itated by the disease of poverty. Standards for physical and mental fitness slackened as the meat grinder of war meant the services had to accept men who were less physically fit, to fill the ranks.

As the war progressed, the army found itself overweight in antiaircraft units—the sacrifice of bombers and their crews over Germany, coupled with the losses of German warplanes, pilots, and synthetic-fuel-production capacity, left the skies relatively safe in the European war's closing months. Personnel from antiaircraft units were often converted into infantry-men, drivers, or whatever position the Army needed to fill.

With more than four hundred thousand Axis POWs in the United States by the end of the war in Europe, men were needed to serve as guards and staff for hundreds of POW camps scattered across the country. Many of those camps were in remote regions of the West where German and Italian prisoners of war contributed to the U.S. war effort by replacing agricultural workers. Most knew that they would be heading home when the war ended at some unknown date in the future. The men guarding and supervising the POWs were often those who were too old to serve on the fronts, had been injured in the fighting, or were otherwise unfit to fight.

Private Clarence V. Bertucci was of the latter category. Bertucci enlisted in the Army in 1940 and was later stationed with an artillery unit in England but proved to be a heavy drinker who was frequently disciplined for military infractions or hospitalized for behavioral issues. The war in Europe ended without Bertucci having made it into the fighting. Instead he had been assigned to stateside duty at Camp Salina in Utah, watching over German POWs. On the night of July 7, 1945, he headed into Salina to liquor up. Before stumbling back to camp, he stopped by Mom's Cafe for a cup of Joe and to tell a waitress "something exciting was going to happen." Shortly after midnight on July 8, he clamored up into a guard tower, got behind the trigger of a .30-caliber machine gun, and raked tents in which German prisoners were soundly sleeping after a hard day of labor in the surrounding beet fields.

"Get more ammo—I'm not done yet!" Bertucci screamed before being subdued by other GIs. Nine Germans were murdered and another score wounded by Bertucci. The dead were later buried at Fort Douglas Military Cemetery near Salt Lake City with full military honors.

The Army had court-martial for Bertucci, who was found insane. Whether he met the legal definition of insanity (not knowing the nature or consequences of his actions) is debatable. Instead of a rope around his neck, the sadistic sad sack was institutionalized for years before being released. He died in 1969, more forgotten than his victims.

In 2016, a museum opened in Salina commemorating the victims of what was known as "Midnight Massacre," as well as Camp Salina's earlier history as a Civilian Conservation Corps camp.

CHAPTER FIVE
The Colditz Cock

"The moment you doubt whether you can fly, you cease for ever to be able to do it."

—J. M. Barrie, Peter Pan

The greatest escape plan of them all—if ingenuity and audacity are the standards—was hatched by the POWs of Colditz Castle, which of course became the subject of a film, albeit a 1971 made-for-TV movie titled *The Birdmen*. Being an ABC Movie of the Week, the decision was made by the producers and writers to plug in American actor Doug McClure as the lead. American television viewers were unlikely to watch a bunch of foreigners pretend to be heroic. To spice up the plot a bit, McClure was an OSS agent tasked with spiriting a Norwegian physicist, played by Rene Auberjonois, out of occupied Europe. Instead, the pair are captured and sent to a castle the Germans have converted into a POW camp. Why not throw in TV veterans Chuck Connors (*The Rifleman*) as another U.S. airman and Richard Basehart (*Voyage to the Bottom of the Sea*) as the commandant of Beckstadt Castle? The POWs then hatch a daring plot to get the physicist out of the escape-proof bastion.

The real and much different events occurred at Colditz Castle, officially designated Oflag IV-C, a high-security prison where Royal Air Force and U.S. Army Air Force flyers made up the majority of prisoners. Many were there because of previous attempts to escape other stalags. Regardless of any claims or reputation for being escape-proof, eleven British POWs made the home run from Colditz, one by walking out in a guard's uniform. Many more were recaptured and at least one prisoner was shot dead in the attempt.

Instead of tunneling or sneaking out in disguise, three prisoners hit on the idea of flying over the prison walls by launching a glider from the chapel roof high above the Mulde River. Lieutenant Tony Rolt came up with the idea, and Flight Lieutenants Bill Goldfinch and Jack Best designed the glider, aided by *Aircraft Design*, a two-volume book the Nazis were good enough to have among the collection in the prison library. To be fair, would the Nazis really expect enemy soldiers imprisoned in a castle to seriously contemplate an escape by air? It would have been a greater concern to the jailers if *The Complete Idiot's Guide to Homemade Automatic Weapons* was on a library shelf.

Rolt, an auto racer before and after the war, was the right man to spearhead the plan. Since his capture in France in 1940, he had escaped from other camps seven times, only to be recaptured and eventually sent to Colditz. On second thought, the Germans might have considered that they had populated the barracks with aviators, men schooled in the piloting and engineering skills that made flight possible.

Aircraft-grade aluminum tubing, fabrics, adhesives, cables, and other ideal materials were not to be found in the stalag, so the inmates scrounged and innovated: Spars, ribs, and struts were fashioned from floorboards, bed slats, and anything else that might not be missed by the guards; gingham bed sheets gave the cock its checkerboard skin; and electrical wire served as the cock's control cables. Those gingham sheets needed to be stiffened, so the prisoners boiled their millet-seed porridge into a varnish to coat the fabric surfaces of the wings and fuselage. The plan called for launching the cock from the chapel roof, setting up a rail-and-pulley system with a concrete-filled bathtub as the counterweight.

Best, Goldfinch, and their assistants hid their project behind a false wall in the attic of the barracks chapel, as a few dozen others served as lookouts while work was in progress. Meanwhile, the U.S. Army was rolling up what was left of the Wehrmacht and liberated the camp on April 16, 1945. This saved Best, Goldfinch, or whoever drew the short straws from riding the two-man craft—a chance at almost certain death or maiming injury with the end of the war in Europe just weeks away. The liberating Americans did get a photograph of the cock before the locals busted it up for firewood, and it looked airworthy, though it was never put to the test—until sixty-seven years later.

In 2012, a British television network sponsored an experiment to determine if the cock had any chance of taking flight and sailing to safety from the fortress roof. As best they could, a team of aeronautical experts assembled a glider to the specifications of the cock, down to the millet-seed porridge. Two major differences existed: Instead of a pilot and a passenger, it was manned by a dummy—literally. A man with a remote radio set controlled the aircraft from a safe distance. The cock flew nearly one thousand feet—and over the Mulde River— before the controller intentionally crashed the craft, mindful of not damaging private property. The reproduction was a crumpled mess of splintered wood and canvas, and the mannequin pilot, well, he was decapitated.

Bold as the plan was to launch two men off a chapel roof more than one hundred feet above ground, one has to wonder: Was the cock a serious escape plan, or a way to relieve the privation and boredom—and restore a sense of mission—of those who cooked up the idea?

By the way, in the best Hollywood tradition, the escape was successful in *The Birdmen*.

CHAPTER SIX
All in the Family

"I will always be the political prisoner of my father's name."

—Svetlana Alliluyeva

You cannot pick your parents, and it is hard to step outside of their shadows, especially if Dad happens to be the ruthless dictator of the Soviet Union. Alliluyeva emerged from Josef Stalin's shadow for a time after her defection to the United States in 1967, but it was the beginning of a long, strange journey as a minor celebrity and best-selling autobiographer that ended in near obscurity in Wisconsin.

"You can't regret your fate," Alliluyeva once said, "although I do regret my mother didn't marry a carpenter."

Stalin's "Little Sparrow" led an unsettled life in America, marrying and divorcing, living a part of that time on a commune. She later renounced her denunciations of the Soviet Union and moved back to her homeland for years before becoming an international transient. Alliluyeva died in 2011 at the age of eighty-five in Wisconsin, where she had lived under her married name of Lana Peters.

Soviet Dictator Josef Stalin in a tender moment with daughter Svetlana in 1937. The relationship would grow colder as the war progressed.

Svetlana's mother, Stalin's second wife, committed suicide when her daughter was six years old. Dad, the murderer of millions, was apparently a doting, even spoiling, father to young Svetlana, although the relationship became more distant as the survival of the Soviet Union in World War II became his focus, according to her *New York Times* obituary. Stalin was also a controlling parent, trying to dictate his daughter's love life and career. When one is a dictator, one can send a daughter's unwanted boyfriend to Siberia.

Alliluyeva's life was no Disney movie, but it was longer and, in the end, less of a tragedy than the lives of her brothers.

Yakov Dzhugashvili (that was Stalin's real last name) was apparently despised by a father who saw him as weak. "He can't even shoot straight," Stalin reportedly said after Yakov's failed suicide attempt. Yakov's luck was all bad. He joined the Red Army as a lieutenant in 1941, just in time for the Nazi invasion in June of that year. A month later, Yakov was a prisoner of the Germans, and Dad was not sympathetic.

"There are no prisoners of war, only traitors to their homeland," Dad supposedly remarked. The Nazis used Yakov's capture as propaganda fodder, dropping the news on leaflets to the Red Army. Later, as the Third Reich's fortunes turned, they tried to use him as bait for a prisoner swap. Field Marshal Friedrich Paulus led the German Sixth Army and hundreds of thousands of its soldiers to defeat, surrender, and miserable deaths at Stalingrad. For some reason, the Nazis wanted Paulus back and offered Yakov in trade.

"I will not trade a marshal for a lieutenant," was the reply from the ultimate practitioner of tough love. Yakov died April 14, 1943, in the Sachsenhausen concentration camp, although there are differing stories as to the circumstances of his death. At one time he was reported to have been the victim of a typhus outbreak. He was later thought to have died trying to escape. Still later, after learning his father ordered the 1940 murder of Polish officers at Katyn Forest, a despondent Yakov ended his life by throwing himself on an electrified fence. The latest, and presumably accurate, account is provided by British historians privy to German records, which state Yakov was shot in the head for disobeying orders from a German guard. Dad would have been proud.

Josef Stalin's son, Yakov, fell into the hands of the German Army in the early months of the Nazi Invasion. He would die in a POW camp in 1943, his father having refused German offers to trade him for a field marshal in Soviet captivity.

Stalin's younger son, Vasily Dzhugashvili, did not suffer as his brother did but must have also been a disappointment to Joe. The kind of kid who might yell, "Do you know who my father is?" in a bar, Vasily was not shy about trading on Dad's name for undeserved military promotions in the Red Air Force, advancing to lieutenant general by the age twenty-five. As Vasily feared, his circumstances declined precipitously shortly after his father's death in 1953. On charges of misappropriation of air force funds (or seeming too chummy with a foreign diplomat), Vasily was tried, convicted, and sentenced to prison. He was released from confinement and officially rehabilitated in 1960, receiving a pension, a Moscow flat, and permission to wear his uniform and decorations.

Freedom did not last long for Vasily. After years of alcohol abuse, he died in 1962, a couple of days short of his forty-first birthday.

****

Benito Mussolini's long reign as the fascist dictator of Italy ended with his bullet-riddled and mangled body hanging by the heels at a Milan gas station. That ignominious end was just desserts for Il Duce, but one of his sons gained a modicum of fame for something other than being a dictator's son.

Future jazz pianist Guilio Romano Mussolini was seventeen when Benito Mussolini was assassinated by Italian partisans. His father had been on the run with his mistress, Clara Petacci, in the waning days of the war, separating from his wife and children in hope they would not meet the fate he feared was awaiting him.

Romano was a child of privilege, and most of his memories of his father and childhood were pleasant ones. Il Duce's last words to Romano, eleven days before his assassination, were "Keep playing," according to the son's 2011 obituary in the *Telegraph*.

Romano had taught himself to play piano and later performed under a pseudonym for a number of years after the war. He dropped the phony name in the 1950s to perform as Romano Mussolini. It seems not to have harmed his career: Romano played with Ella Fitzgerald and jammed with Louis Armstrong and Lionel Hampton. Sophia Loren's younger sister, Maria Sciccolone, sang in his band, and their dozen-year marriage produced two daughters, one of whom became a member of the European Parliament representing a conservative Italian political party.

Romano outlived his reviled father by almost sixty-one years, dying in 2006 at the age of seventy-eight. Early in his musical career, he was reluctant to use the last name Mussolini when performing but rose above an infamous surname to claim a reputation of his own.

****

On July 4, 1939, two months before the invasion of Poland kicked off the war in Europe, *Look* magazine published "Why I Hate My Uncle," by William Hitler.

"I was struck by his intensity, his feminine gestures. There was dandruff on his coat," Billy Hitler wrote about Uncle Adolf. Then the nephew really let loose on his uncle. Among the article's scathing accusations was that Der Führer had impregnated his half-niece Geli Raubal, "a fact that enraged Hitler. His revolver was found by her body." Raubal's death in an apparent suicide in 1931 was well known in Germany, as was Hitler's apparent infatuation with the twenty-three-year-old woman.

After articles Bill wrote about Adolf were published in Britain, he was summoned to Berlin where Hitler "was furious. Pacing up and down, wild-eyed and tearful, he made me promise to retract my articles and threatened to kill himself if anything else were written about his private life."

Born in Liverpool in 1911, William Patrick Hitler was the son of Adolf Hitler's half-brother, Alois, and his first wife, Bridget (Dowling) Hitler. Alois was not much of a father, abandoning his family three years later and returning to Europe. He later remarried without benefit of a divorce from the first Mrs. Hitler.

William visited his father in Germany in 1929, but soon returned to England. However, he came back to Germany in 1933, at which time his uncle helped him out financially, getting him a job at a bank and later with the automaker Opal. For a few years, he bounced back and forth between jobs in England and Germany. Despite an apparently contentious relationship with his uncle, William Hitler might have played on Hitler's power and fame to his advantage in Germany, but the name recognition did not help his job prospects in Great Britain, unless he was dissing and dishing on Adolf.

One cannot pick blood relatives, and the underlying relationship between Adolf and William was that of rich uncle to a poor relation. William likely saw an opportunity to get a leg up in life through his association with the new chancellor of Germany. Adolf Hitler might have seen Billy as the ne'er-do-well son of a half-brother with whom he had a limited relationship but still felt some familial obligation. Possibly the murderer of millions felt he had to put in a good word for his brother's kid.

As the *Look* article would illustrate, Bill's relationship with Uncle Adolf was fractious. William Hitler was even jailed for a time during the 1934 purge in which Ernst Röhm and other Brownshirt leaders were rounded up and executed, according to a 2014 French documentary.

As tensions rose in Europe and his connection with the dictator deteriorated, William gave up on making his mark in the Third Reich. Back in England, he and mother Bridget embarked for America. Bill benefited from a William Randolph Hearst–sponsored speaking tour of the United States and that *Look* article. After Pearl Harbor, William tried to enlist, but was refused. He eventually made a personal appeal to President Roosevelt by letter and in 1944 became a U.S. Navy pharmacist's mate. Hitler was wounded by shrapnel and received the Purple Heart, according to several articles, though they included no details of the action.

Whether his motivation to join the military was altruistic, patriotic, or something less noble is just speculation. Regardless, he served along with sixteen million others in U.S. armed forces. After the war, Bill was no longer willing to bear the surname of the century's greatest mass murderer and legally changed his name to William Stuart-Houston. He got married, raised a family on Long Island, and passed away at the age of seventy-six in 1987.

That 2014 French documentary, *The Pact* (*Les serment des Hitler*) sheds light on why Billy chose Stuart-Houston to replace Hitler as his last name. The explanation shows the nephew's differences with his uncle might have been more personal than philosophical. Houston and Stewart (note the different spelling) were the first and middle names of a British-born writer and philosopher who emigrated to Germany and married Richard Wagner's daughter. Houston Stewart Chamberlain died in 1927 but not before establishing a correspondence and meeting with Adolf Hitler, by then the leader of the fledgling NSDAP. In the years following World War I, Chamberlain scapegoated Jews and the United States for Germany having lost the Great War. If that was unintentional on William Hitler's part, it would be a strange coincidence.

The documentary claims William Hitler's children entered into a pact never to have children, although William Hitler's surviving sons (one had died in a car crash) declined to be interviewed.

****

Once a decade or so, a newspaper or magazine article documents a sighting of Arthur MacArthur IV, son of General Douglas MacArthur. In March 2014, the *Daily Mail* reported the general's son was living under another name in the Mayflower Hotel in New York City. Developers were buying out the last four tenants in the rent-controlled building, but some were demanding big checks to relocate. One elderly man held out for a mind-boggling $17 million. MacArthur agreed to move to Greenwich Village for a mere $650,000.

Some children trade on the fame or fortune of a parent. For reasons of his own, Arthur MacArthur decided to step out of the long shadow cast by the "American Caesar" and live an almost anonymous life as a musician. But in the first few years of his life, Arthur was among the most famous children in America outside of Hollywood, except he was not in America.

Dad retired from the U.S. Army and took a job as the military advisor to the Philippine government. The general's wife, Jean, gave birth to Arthur in 1938. With war looming, MacArthur was recalled to active duty to command U.S. forces in the Philippines in July 1941. Within hours of the attack on Pearl Harbor, the Japanese invaded the Philippines and quickly rolled up the native and American forces.

With American and Philippine forces fighting, starving, and dying on the Bataan Peninsula, General MacArthur, Jean, and young Arthur were across Manila Bay on—and inside—the island fortress of Corregidor. In one of the most famous—or infamous—escapes of the war, MacArthur, his family, and key members of his staff—including Arthur's Chinese nanny—boarded PT boats to avoid what would have been certain capture or death in the island's tunnels and a huge propaganda coup for Japan. MacArthur and his entourage were later evacuated by air to Australia where he was named supreme Allied commander, southwest Pacific area.

Young Arthur was pictured on magazine covers and was accompanied by an armed escort wherever he went. Decades after the war, former Staff Sgt. E. F. "Jerry" Germaine, a member of the Australian Women's Army Service, penned an article for an Australian publication about her time as a member of General MacArthur's office staff in Brisbane. In it, she recalled an encounter with Jean and young Arthur as she walked a friend's German shepherd in a park.

"When four-year-old Arthur MacArthur stretched out an arm to pat Prince . . . the two U.S. Army sergeants guarding General Douglas MacArthur's wife and young son drew their pistols, ready to shoot the dog if it as much as licked the boy's hand," Germaine wrote. Jean MacArthur recognized Germaine from her husband's staff, and from that time on the sergeants knew not to draw down on Jerry.

In 1950 Oscar Samuel Roloff was serving on a press team for Vice Admiral Turner Joy in Tokyo when he had his Arthur MacArthur sighting. He wrote about it years later for the *Woodinville Weekly* in Washington State:

One day, (General MacArthur) ruled that his son, Arthur, 12, would take a warship ride from Yokosuka to Tokyo. Col. S. C. Huff, aide de camp to the General, was ordered to go along and watch the kid's every move, to protect him. . . . I watched the lad, who seemed entirely uninterested, ill at ease, as he sat on a forward bitt [bollard]. No sailor was allowed to talk to him.

Roloff concluded from watching and photographing Arthur that "The kid wanted to march to a different drummer—not his Dad's drum." Arthur would not be going to West Point, graduating instead from Columbia University.

Those two snapshots from Arthur's childhood could lead amateur psychologists to surmise that he lived not just a sheltered youth but also an isolated one. Douglas and Jean doted over their only child, and as the son of one of the world's most famous men, they reasonably feared he could be targeted by kidnappers or assassins.

Despite occasionally surfacing in a magazine or newspaper article, the adult Arthur MacArthur has for the most part been able to successfully guard his privacy.

****

Not all World War II leaders produced children with odd, unusual, or tragic stories. Franklin and Eleanor Roosevelt had six children, five of whom would live to adulthood. The four sons all served the armed forces during the war: James joined the Marine Corps, saw combat with the Marine Raiders, was awarded a Silver Star, and retired a brigadier general; Elliott joined the Army Air Corps, flew scores of combat missions, and, likewise, became a brigadier general; Franklin Jr. saw combat in the Atlantic and Pacific, rose to the rank of lieutenant commander in the Navy, and commanded a destroyer escort; and John Roosevelt was also a Navy man, seeing combat on the carrier USS *Wasp*, receiving a Bronze Star and promotion to lieutenant commander.

None of the Roosevelt boys hid themselves behind Dad's wheelchair to avoid serving, although John considered seeking conscientious-objector status. If anything, they parlayed the family name to avoid cushy, noncombat, rear echelon assignments.

Ike's son, John S. D. Eisenhower, graduated from the U.S. Military Academy in 1944 and served in Europe during the war. Generals Omar Bradley and George Patton were apparently leery of putting their boss's son in danger, so John was given staff assignments. John Eisenhower did see combat in the Korean War and went on to be an advisor to his father during his presidency, ambassador to Belgium (during the Nixon administration), and a respected historian and author.

John Eisenhower may have best summed up what it is like to be the son of a historic figure: "I was patted on the head as the great man's son," he told *USA Today* in a 1989 interview. "I said: 'The hell with it. I'm going to get into something my old man couldn't get into.'"

CHAPTER SEVEN

The Other (More Interesting) Churchill

"An officer who goes into action without his sword is improperly dressed."

—Jack Churchill

In nine decades spanning from Queen Victoria's reign over the world's largest empire through Great Britain's precipitous fall in stature and influence by the 1960s, Winston Churchill's life was one of almost unparalleled adventure and accomplishment. A short list would include the following:

- Cavalryman with Lord Kitchener's forces in Sudan.
- War correspondent, prisoner of war, and escapee during the Boer War.
- Longtime member of Parliament.

- First lord of the admiralty in two world wars and a battalion commander during the Great War.
- Twice prime minister.
- Nobel laureate in literature.

Winston's life was not always on an upward trajectory of success: He was forced to resign as first lord of the admiralty in World War I, in part because of the Gallipoli disaster against the Ottomans in Turkey. His penance was to ask for the Western Front battalion command. Having shepherded his nation through the darkest days of the Second World War through to victory, the British people voted him out of office while he was attending the Potsdam Conference with Stalin and Truman. A historical nonentity, Labor Party leader Clement Attlee got to finish off the conference, with Stalin likely wondering what the hell happened to his drinking companion.

There was another Churchill who lived a life that, if not as impactful as the prime minister's, rivaled that of many a literary or cinematic hero: Lt. Colonel John Malcolm Thorpe Fleming Churchill, better known among his colleagues as "Fighting Jack" and "Mad Jack." One quote from a fellow officer in the commandos, Peter Young, gives some hint of the man:

> Major Churchill disappeared, sword in hand, into the thick smoke, uttering warlike cries. No braver man fought at Vaagso that day, a gallant man to follow into action, though decidedly conservative in his military ideas. He is the only man, to the certain knowledge of the present writer, who has transfixed a German with an arrow from a longbow—but that is another story.

If by conservative Young meant the fifteenth century, that fit Mad Jack like a suit of armor, as he went into some battles armed with both longbow and claymore, while also weighed down by modern arms and ordnance. Or sometimes he announced his arrival in battle by playing the bagpipes, at which he was quite accomplished. Churchill was playing "March of the Cameron Men" as British Commando No. 3 approached the shores of Vaagso, Norway—not the best way to sneak up on the enemy. Churchill, second in command of the battalion, can be seen in one photograph wading through the icy surf (it was December 27, 1941) clutching the sword in his right hand. A photograph from later in the raid shows Fighting Jack with a dirk or dagger slipped into his waistband.

Seen here at the end of the war, "Mad Jack" Churchill still had the look of a man ready, willing, and able to skewer his enemies with a long bow.

Churchill's battalion was charged with neutralizing the German artillery on the nearby island of Maaloy, allowing the other units to deal with the German garrison at Vaasgo, damage and destroy shipping and fish-processing factories, and bring back any Norwegians willing to aid the Allied cause. In photographs taken during the action, a longbow and quiver are noticeably absent from Churchill's shoulder, despite the Vaasgo raid having the code name Operation Archery. Such raids did not cause great damage and disruption to the German occupiers, but they did keep several divisions and Luftwaffe units tied up in the north when they could have been more usefully employed on the eastern or western fronts.

The skewering of the German soldier took place about a year and a half prior to the raid on Vaasgo and is, as Young wrote, another story.

Born in Ceylon (now Sri Lanka) in 1906, John was one of three sons to civil-service engineer Alec Churchill and his wife, Elinor. The couple's two other sons, Thomas Bell Lindsay Churchill and Robert Alec Farquhar Churchill, also served in the war. Jack graduated from the Royal Military College, Sandhurst, in 1926, after which he was packed off to serve with a battalion of the Manchester Regiment in Burma. During his time there, he explored that country and parts of India on a Zenith motorcycle. Without commenting on the quality of British motor vehicles, his long journeys were more than challenging. The roads and cart paths he traveled were often better suited to water buffaloes than motorbikes.

The dearth of suitable roads often forced Churchill to travel along railway rights-of-way to get around. This was a particularly tricky piece of motorcycle riding—or pushing—on trestles and bridges where there was nothing but air between the railroad ties. Petrol stations must have been almost nonexistent in the subcontinent of the later 1920s and early 1930s.

Jack Churchill became proficient in two skills, or obsessions, that would be woven into his legend: archery and the bagpipes. After a decade in the peacetime military, he left the British Army and showed off those skills. Having learned to play the bagpipes from a Scottish pipe major while assigned to the Manchester Regiment in Burma, he placed second on that instrument in the 1938 Aldershot Military Tattoo, an event featuring military musical performances, parades, and competitions. At the 1939 World Archery Championships held in Oslo, Norway, Churchill was a member of the British team.

In the years before the war, Churchill put his chiseled features to use from time to time as a male model in Kenya, while also earning a few pounds as a newspaper editor. Years earlier, he supposedly put that face of his to work as an extra in the 1924 Douglas Fairbanks Sr. version of *The Thief of Bagdad*, although that would have placed an eighteen-year-old Churchill in Los Angeles, California. More easily verifiable is his appearance as an archer—great typecasting—in MGM's 1952 epic blockbuster *Ivanhoe*, with Robert Taylor. Much of the movie's exteriors were filmed in England, so Churchill's role is in little doubt.

With the outbreak of war in 1939, Churchill was back in uniform and with the British Expeditionary Force in France for the *Sitzkrieg*, the period of quiet on the western front in late 1939 and early 1940 before the Wehrmacht launched its blitzkrieg in May. When the Germans unleashed their ground forces and Luftwaffe that spring, they quickly rolled up the French Army and BEF, eventually pinning four hundred thousand Allied troops against the English Channel at Dunkirk. The incident that turbocharged Churchill's reputation for reckless bravery and eccentricity purportedly took place during the fighting retreat toward the sea.

On May 27, 1940, then-Captain Jack Churchill was with his company defending the village of L'Epinette. From his vantage point in a tower, he spotted a small group of German soldiers taking cover behind the stone wall of a farmyard. Picking out a sergeant, Churchill told one of his comrades, "I will shoot that first German with an arrow." Drawing one from his quiver, he sent it streaking into the German's chest to signal the beginning of the ambush. One account then has him wading into the general melee, carving his way through a wall of German flesh before dispatching another pair of Huns with his sidearm.

Or, in another account, Churchill spots a group of German soldiers hiding in a distant thicket and sends a pair of arrows their way with uncertain results.

Were these separate events, or very different versions of the same incident? Jack's fellow commando Young, who became a brigadier general, was quite convinced of the truth of the story of the transfixed German soldier. Further supporting evidence that something like the longbow kill occurred was an eyewitness account from shortly before the British evacuation. As the BEF was pushed into the Dunkirk pocket, a soldier recorded seeing Churchill cruising the beach on a motorcycle, longbow and quiver over his shoulder, a German soldier's cap affixed to one end of the bow.

Whether or not he speared an enemy soldier, Jack Churchill had performed enough feats of bravery in France to acquire the monikers "Fighting Jack" and "Mad Jack." Once safely in England, he wasted no time in volunteering for the commandos, training in the Scottish Highlands at Achnacarry. Through his exploits in Norway and onto Italy and Yugoslavia, Churchill's reputation for audacity—or foolhardiness—grew. One description of his going ashore in Sicily in 1943 conjures up a picture more like that of Peter Sellers invading New York City in *The Mouse that Roared* than Arnold Schwarzenegger arming up in *Commando*.

Churchill was seen leading No. 2 Commando "with his trademark Scottish broadsword strapped around his waist, a longbow and arrows around his neck, and his bagpipes under his arm." There's no mention of a Sten gun or Enfield rifle. Mad Jack might have used the archaic weaponry and ear-piercing wail of the pipes to pump up the spirits of his own troops while sowing fear in the hearts of the enemy, but there are plenty of good reasons to have left them behind: A clattering sword and scabbard do not lend themselves to stealth, and a longbow and quiver would likely keep getting caught on branches, limbs, and other obstructions. The racket bagpipes make is explanation enough as to why they are rarely used for anything but assaulting people's eardrums at ceremonial events.

In a contested Italian village, Fighting Jack, wielding only his broadsword, bluffed more than forty Germans into surrendering to him and a (presumably better-armed) corporal. From there he was assigned to command a reinforced unit that included No. 43 Royal Marine Commando, along with a company of light infantry and an artillery unit to bolster Yugoslav partisans. To this point in the war, Jack's fortunes held, having survived many firefights, bullet and shrapnel wounds, and other close calls. That luck ran short in a 1944 attack on a German-held island in the Adriatic. Isolated from the main body of his force with only a handful of men, all of whom were to be killed or wounded, Churchill, true to form, fired off his last round before advancing on the Germans playing "Will Ye No Come Back Again?" on the pipes. The Germans responded to the serenade with a grenade and a wounded Churchill became a prisoner of war.

Winston Churchill had a younger brother, John, known as "Jack," which might have confused Mad Jack's captors into thinking they had bagged a relative of the prime minister. For bad or worse, he was sent to Sachsenhausen concentration camp, which housed a number of high-profile prisoners, among them the July 20 plotters and sympathizers and others of whom Hitler had grown weary or wary. Churchill and an RAF officer escaped by going under the wire in September 1944, but they were recaptured near the Baltic Sea coast and returned to Sachsenhausen. In the closing weeks of the war, as the Red Army pushed in from the east, Churchill was among a group of prisoners sent from Germany to another camp in Austria near the Italian border.

Being in the custody of an SS unit, the captives feared they would be executed as the Allies closed in. Leaders of the group were able to convince a regular German Army unit to replace the SS guards, who were outnumbered and took the hint to hand over the prisoners. Churchill's second "escape" was more akin to violating house arrest, as the new guards were more interested in seeing the war end than committing a few last war crimes. Rather than wait it out until the Allies arrived, Fighting Jack began a nearly one-hundred-mile trek across the Alps through the Brenner Pass and into Italy where he met up with an advancing U.S. Army armor column near Verona.

There was still a war raging on in the Pacific and, after some time to recuperate, Jack saw no reason to miss out on the remaining fighting to be done in the Far East. The war ended while he was in India, training with a commando unit set to fight in his old stomping grounds of Burma. Most everyone considered the end of the war a good thing, except for Mad Jack, who was quoted as saying, "If it weren't for those damn Yanks, we could have kept the war going for another ten years!"

Even a warrior as eccentric—or maniacal—as Churchill might have thought differently had he gone through a few months of warfare in the wretched jungle conditions of Burma, where disease and the drenching, rotting climate were enemies nearly as fearsome as the Japanese. Riding a motor-cycle through a backward country in peacetime is one thing; fighting a fanatical enemy in a trackless jungle is another.

Six years of war had left Britain financially broken and worn at its imperial edges—an empire that largely disinte-grated over the next two decades. Still, Fighting Jack found adventure in the postwar years, taking his first parachute jump on his fortieth birthday and commanding an airborne battal-ion. Two years later, as second in command of the Highland Light Infantry, Jack was stationed in Palestine, then in its last days as a British mandate. There, Churchill showed he was just as capable of saving lives as he had been at ending them a few years before. On April 13, 1948, Arab fighters ambushed a convoy of Jewish medical personnel headed for Hadassah Hospital in Jerusalem. Churchill attempted to intervene, with one British soldier being killed, and evacuated some of the Jewish doctors, nurses, and orderlies. Most in the convoy chose to go forward, expecting escort and protection from the Haganah. Instead, seventy-seven of the medical personnel were killed in what became known as the Hadassah Medical Convoy Massacre. Churchill's men later helped evacuate some five hundred or more patients and staff from Hadassah Hospital in the massacre's aftermath.

Toward the end of his military career, Lieutenant Colonel Churchill was posted to Australia and found a new obsession—surfing. He returned to England, where he was assigned to a desk job, but showed some of his old flash by surfing the tidal bore of the River Severn for more than a mile.

Mad Jack married Rosamund Denny, the daughter of a Scottish shipbuilder, during the war, and together they raised two sons. Malcolm Churchill described a father who rarely gave into braggadocio over his exploits, other than with a good friend over a bottle of wine. Mad Jack enjoyed refurbishing eleven steamboats to ply the River Thames and building and selling remote-control model boats. Jack and Rosamund lived a peaceful life in the postwar years, but as a middle-aged commuter he would occasionally astonish fellow train passengers by tossing his briefcase out of the window. Little did they know he was throwing it into his own back garden adjacent to the tracks.

John Churchill was eighty-nine years old when he died in 1996, and by then it had become difficult to separate the facts from the fictions of his life. The longbow story appears to have several versions, and obituaries and articles list his birthplace as either Ceylon, Surrey, or Hong Kong. The latter two are where his brothers, Thomas and Robert, were born.

Major General Thomas Bell Lindsay Churchill was also a distinguished commando leader during the war, joining in 1942, a year after his older brother Jack. He commanded 2nd Commando Brigade in Italy and later served in Yugoslavia, supporting Josip Broz Tito's partisans, where he was also Jack's superior officer. For Tom, the war ended in Albania, where he captured the port of Sarande from the Germans. In peacetime, Tom Churchill rose to serve in a number of high staff positions in the British Army. Postwar, he served as commander of the British Zone in Austria and later as quartermaster general to the Forces at the War Office. His last assignment was deputy chief of staff, Allied Land Forces, Europe. He retired in 1962.

Robert Alec Farquhar Churchill served with the Fleet Air Arm. Known as "Buster," Alec Churchill served with 884 Squadron on the aircraft carrier HMS *Victorious* as it tried to shepherd merchantmen loaded with essential food, supplies, and ordnance bound for the embattled Mediterranean island of Malta in the summer of 1942. Operation Pedestal succeeded— barely—and at a high cost in British warships, merchant vessels, aircraft, and lives. In the confines of the Mediterranean Sea, the Royal Navy was vulnerable to attack from land-based enemy aircraft from Italy and Axis-occupied countries and territories. Hundreds of German and Italian aircraft, backed by torpedo boats and submarines, swarmed the convoy, protected only by its antiaircraft guns and just seventy-four fighters from four aircraft carriers. Buster Churchill was shot down and killed on August 12, 1942.

****

After the Royal Navy sank the *Bismarck* in May 1941, the British remained wary that its sister ship, *Tirpitz*, might break out into the North Atlantic and use its fifteen-inch guns to pummel the convoys that were Britain's lifeline to North America (despite the much greater threat posed by the U-boats of the Kriegsmarine). In June 1942 the rumor that Tirpitz left its anchorage resulted in a panicked British admiralty ordering Convoy PQ-17 to scatter—and become easy prey for the U-boats. Twenty-four of the thirty-five merchant ships in the convoy went to the bottom.

The British worried that, should Tirpitz sally forth from the Norwegian fjords where it sheltered, the 45,500-ton battleship might find safe harbor in the occupied French port of Saint-Nazaire, home to a mammoth drydock that could serve the battleship should it need repairs.

To deny Tirpitz use of the drydock, Loud Mountbatten approved a plan to ram an obsolete, explosives-laden American Lend Lease destroyer into the lock gates. The *Campbeltown*, a World War I–vintage four-stacker, was cut down to give it a profile more resembling a German destroyer, and its bow was packed with five tons of high explosives. The plan worked, at high cost to the Royal Navy, the commandos who manned *Campbeltown*, and a small fleet of escorting motor launches, a motor gunboat, a motor torpedo boat, and four escorting destroyers.

In the predawn hours of March 28, 1942, *Campbeltown* breached the gates as commandos in the converted destroyer and the escorting motor launches scrambled ashore to set demolition charges to other dockyard machinery. The time-delayed fuse on *Campbeltown* went off at about 10 a.m., blowing up the ship and the German soldiers who had gathered to inspect the damage to the lock.

Of the 611 commandos and sailors who embarked on the mission, 169 were killed, and scores of others spent the rest of the war in captivity. Winston Churchill and Mountbatten would top that carnage in August when they sent a mostly Canadian force to be slaughtered in an amphibious raid with the goal of temporarily holding the port of Dieppe. Half of the six thousand Canadians and other forces that landed at Dieppe were killed, wounded, or captured—for nothing.

Mountbatten would continue to fail upward in his career, later becoming supreme Allied commander in the China-Burma-India theater. Until the day he was blown up by an Irish Republican Army bomb on his fishing boat in 1979, he would not admit the failure of the Dieppe raid, or anything else, for that matter. If anyone was at fault, Mountbatten believed it was Field Marshal Bernard Law Montgomery, who he said (perhaps with justification in this case) tampered with Mountbatten's operational plan for the raid before heading off to North Africa in the months prior to El Alamein.

"It is a curious thing, but a fact, that I have been right in everything I have done and said in my life," Lord Louis is quoted in *Mountbatten: A Biography*, by Richard Hough. A healthy ego is essential to good leadership. A sense of infallibility is a severe handicap.

To what end were the sailors and commandos sacrificed at Saint-Nazaire? *Tirpitz* had steamed to Norway in January 1942 and spent its service life hiding from British bombers and guarding against X-craft midget submarines, never confronting enemy vessels in the open sea. In one brief foray into the North Atlantic, *Tirpitz* was attacked by carrier-borne torpedo bombers but escaped back to Norway without damage. Torpedo bombers knocked out *Bismarck's* steering the year before, making it easy meat for Royal Navy surface warships. Hitler feared he could lose *Tirpitz* in the same manner, so he opted not to use the behemoth at all. The British continued to send carrier- and land-based aircraft against the battleship. In November 1944, Lancasters struck the ship with three twelve-thousand-pound Tallboys, and Tirpitz capsized, ending a career that was almost all threat and no action.

****

"For great gallantry and inspiring example whilst a prisoner of war in German hands in Norway and afterwards at Sachsenhausen, near Oranienburg, Germany, 1942–1945: Mention in Despatches (Posthumous). Temporary Lieutenant John GODWIN, R.N.V.R."
—The London Gazette, October 9, 1945.

The notice says almost nothing of Godwin's "great gallantry and inspiring example," but he sold his life dearly.

The 25-year-old Godwin was captured in the aftermath of a commando raid by No. 14 (Arctic) Commando on Haugesund, Norway, on April 28, 1943. The commandos were dropped off by a motor torpedo boat at a nearby island from where they paddled canoes to their objective, sinking a minesweeper and some commercial shipping vessels by attaching limpet mines to the hulls.

The commandos made their getaway, but plans for their pickup and return to England went awry when their mother ship failed to show. Godwin and six other commandos were captured in uniform on May 15, 1943, "with the cooperation of Norwegian civilians," according to a German document. Godwin ended up at Sachsenhausen concentration camp, where he suffered the indignities and tortures at which the Nazis excelled.

Hitler issued an order in 1942 for the execution of captured commandos. It took some time, but the Nazis finally decided to execute Godwin and others by firing squad on February 2, 1945. Godwin did not go quietly: He wrestled away the pistol of the soldier in charge of the firing squad and shot him dead before he himself was killed by the other—no doubt astonished—members of the execution detail.

CHAPTER EIGHT

Flight Officer Fester

"Two of them must have thought I was a god."

—Jackie Coogan

Jackie Coogan's career might have peaked when he was six years old, but few people could have experienced as many tragic lows in a lifetime yet still end on a high note. In 1921 he starred alongside Charlie Chaplin in *The Kid*, but his career slumped when he reached adolescence and young adulthood, with some of his adult traits beginning to show: thinning hair, broad mouth, twangy voice, largish nose, and sizable middle-age spread.

Born in 1914, Coogan's life had taken many strange turns by the time he was old enough to vote. Aside from starring in about twenty silent films and a handful of talkies, Coogan had a good friend who was kidnapped and murdered (and likely played a role in lynching the killers), lost his father in a car crash in which he was injured and three other men killed, sued his mother and stepfather for stealing his fortune (and had a law named for him), and got married to and divorced from one of the most beautiful women of his era. Add to that his volunteering for one of the most dangerous jobs in World War II.

By the time he'd hit thirty, Coogan had experienced five lifetimes of heartache and adventure. His iconic role for two seasons as Uncle Fester in the 1960s sitcom *The Addams Family* seems almost an afterthought. Parents and kids who watched the 1964–66 run of this lame-brained comedy mostly knew Coogan only from his role as the bald, portly, and ghoulish uncle who lit up lightbulbs by sticking them in his mouth. In the dim memories of some grandparents in the 1960s, Coogan might have been recalled for his string of silent hits.

John Leslie Coogan entered the world on October 26, 1914, in Los Angeles, the first of two sons born to John Henry Coogan Jr. and Lillian Dolliver Coogan. Dad was in show biz, and Jackie was trodding the boards in vaudeville as soon as he could walk. The boy made his first film at the age of three and landed his breakout role after Chaplin caught his act at a theater. Coogan became a star when he played the adorable abandoned waif to Chaplin's "Little Tramp" character in the comedy-drama *The Kid*.

That hit was followed by *Peck's Bad Boy* (1921), *Oliver Twist* (1922), and other box-office moneymakers. At the height of his fame he was heavily merchandised—one could buy a pail of Jackie Coogan Peanut Butter or dozens of other trinkets and products featuring his endorsement. In 1924 the kid had enough celebrity juice to raise the then-astronomical sum of $1 million for Near East Relief, touring in the United States and later in Europe, where the Irish Catholic was granted an audience with Pope Pius XI.

Jackie got off to a hot start in the talking era, including two performances as Tom Sawyer in *Tom Sawyer* (1930), and *Huckleberry Finn* the following year. The two films were the top-grossing movies for those years. Coogan reportedly earned $4 million as a child actor, but most of that would be gone by the time he was old enough to spend it.

Tragedy struck in 1933 when Coogan's college pal Brooke Hart was kidnapped. A $40,000 ransom was demanded for the 22-year-old department-store heir, but he had already been shot in the head and dumped in San Francisco Bay. Thomas Thurmond and John Holmes were arrested for Hart's murder but were never tried. A mob of thousands gathered outside the San Jose jail where they were being held, and Governor James "Sunny Jim" Rolph refused requests to call out the National Guard. Having gotten the green light, the mob broke in, beat the suspects half senseless, and hung them from a tree across the street in St. James Park. One was naked but for a sock, the other naked from the waist down.

The event was well-covered by the press, with Royce Brier of the *San Francisco Chronicle* being awarded a Pulitzer Prize. It was a well-photographed lynching, as well, with pictures of a gang of men using a post as a battering ram on the jailhouse doors and the crowd gathered around the tree from which Thurmond and Holmes swung. Hart's close friend Jackie Coogan was said to have played a leading role in the killings of the kidnappers, but it was not the type of tidbit press agents routinely put in celebrity bios.

Tragedy struck again on March 4, 1935, when Jackie's dad was behind the wheel of a car that crashed on a country road in San Diego County, killing the father and three other passengers: ranch manager Charles Jones, actor Trent "Junior" Durkin, and writer Robert L. Horner. Riding in the rumble seat, Coogan was himself badly injured. In the inevitable civil trial that followed, Coogan testified his father swerved to avoid another vehicle that was straddling the center of the road, causing the senior Coogan's vehicle to skid out of control and hit a guard post.

As if the loss of his father and friends was not enough of a blow, Jackie later found himself embroiled in a lawsuit with his surviving parent. In 1936, Lillian married her late husband's financial advisor, Arthur Bernstein, and Jackie claimed he was financially cut adrift.

"The young man has received everything he is entitled to," Bernstein's lawyer, Charles Katz, said in a 1938 newspaper interview. "His mother was entitled to all his earning up to the time he came of age."

In the same article, Coogan recalled his mother telling him: "You haven't got a cent. There's never been a cent belonging to you. It's all mine and Arthur's and so far as we are concerned, you will never get a cent."

Long litigation story told short, Coogan was able to get some of what was left of his earnings, somewhere north of $100,000 once he paid his legal bills. The following year, 1939, California passed the Coogan Act requiring that a portion of a child performer's earnings be placed in a blocked trust account.

Amidst all the bad news, Jackie romanced and, in 1937, married Elizabeth Ruth Grable, the first and most famous of his four wives. The following year, the newlyweds paired up in *College Swing*, both in supporting roles as his star was setting and hers rising. They were together on the silver screen again when she was top-billed in 1939's *Million Dollar Legs*. Betty Grable's career had eclipsed Jackie's and they divorced the same year.

Possibly wanting to put the 1930s behind him, Jackie enlisted in the U.S. Army on March 4, 1941, months before Pearl Harbor. Two years later on January 19, 1943, an Associated Press article noted that "the juvenile star of two decades ago is a flight officer in the Army Air Force's gliding school. He was graduated yesterday. Jackie, former husband of Actress Betty Grable, has completed 22 months as an enlisted man in medical, quartermaster's, and anti-tank units. He enlisted as a glider pilot seven months ago."

Thousands of gliders were used, primarily by the Americans and British, to transport airborne troops to objectives. Thousands of Allied troops were killed and injured when the tow planes or gliders were shot out of the air, when gliders were let loose above oceans instead of land, or, more often, in landings. Glider landings might be better described as controlled (and uncontrolled) crashes. The USAAF used wood and canvas Waco CG-4A gliders.

A year after graduating glider school, Flight Officer Coogan found himself stationed in India with the 1st American Air Commando, preparing to go far behind Japanese lines in Burma for a daring campaign of questionable merit. British Major General Orde Wingate was the driving force behind the Chindits, a brigade trained for long-range penetration missions behind enemy lines. In a war of weather extremes, Burma was as awful a battleground as the North Atlantic or Russian steppe in winter, or the year-round jungle stench of Papua-New Guinea, or Guadalcanal in the Pacific. Now called Myanmar, the country lies between the equator and the Tropic of Cancer, with the average high temperature hovering at about 90 degrees in the coastal and Irrawaddy Delta regions. Mountain ranges running north to south are separated by plains, some dense with jungle. In the monsoon regions, rains average upwards of two hundred inches a year. Heat exhaustion, infection, and disease were as likely to kill or disable a soldier as a Japanese bullet.

Into Burma's more mountainous northern region, Wingate planned to land Chindit units by glider to establish a series of fortified bases from which to send out patrols to harass Japanese Army lines of communication. The camps would be supplied by air, so building airstrips was the first order or business after confronting any Japanese units that might be in the vicinity of the landing areas.

The British had conducted aerial reconnaissance of a few clearings where they hoped to land enough gliders with enough Chindits to hold the ground. One, Piccadilly, was covered with felled trees that made landing impossible. It was later revealed that the tree trunks were set out by loggers to cure, not by the Japanese in an effort to deny a landing zone.

The first landing was made at Broadway in early March 1944, and the United Press reported finding a former screen star in the most unlikely of places:

Two decades before he took the role of Uncle Fester on *The Addams Family*, badass Jackie Coogan was piloting gliders and light planes far behind Japanese lines in Burma.

The movie star was Jackie Coogan, "The Kid" who used to roam Hollywood's movie streets 20 years ago. Now Flight Officer Coogan, Jackie was one of the first of the American Glider pilots who landed their troop-jammed craft on the makeshift jungle airstrip some 90 miles south of where Lt. Gen. Stillwell's Chinese and American forces are pushing southward from the Hukawng Valley.

The article, published about two weeks after the landing, reported the Japanese were caught completely by surprise, taking them several days to pinpoint just where the glider force had landed.

It was American C-47 transports (the military version of the twin-engine DC-3) and the American-made Wacos that brought the Chindits in, and before March was over the Associated Press had tracked down Coogan back in India:

Flight Officer Coogan of the American Air Commandos, first glider pilot to land Allied trooper behind Japanese lines in Burma, came back to his base today (March 26) to relate how he was "taken for a god" by native Burmese when they saw him alight in their paddy fields. . . . The former child star, tired and dirty, spent four days in Japanese-occupied Burma on his mission, helping American engineers build a runway for transports which landed with the main body of airborne troops participating in the drive.

Coogan proved a good interview. "If you think the natives were surprised when our gliders landed, you should have seen them when we opened up the mouth of one and drove out a jeep," Coogan told the reporter. "Two of them must have thought I was a god because they followed me everywhere" making him a bed of banana leaves that night.

Coogan related that he brought the glider and its cargo of "British and Gurhka knife artists" in by moonlight to a relatively safe landing. As pilot of the first glider to land, Coogan jumped out of his craft to set flare pots to guide in other gliders filled with British and Indian troops. Thirty-seven of fifty-four gliders made it to Broadway, half a dozen having landed elsewhere in Burma and others having force-landed in British occupied territory. Some 350 men were available to fight, but the cost of landing was steep: about thirty killed and another twenty injured, according to an account by Brigadier Bernard Ferguson.

Ferguson also reported that a dozen light planes, probably Stinson L-5s, arrived during the day, and a USAAF major offered to fly out the wounded. Ferguson's description indicated Coogan, a civilian pilot before the war, lent a hand: "This was our first experience of these very gallant light plane pilots, one of whom was Sergeant Jackie Coogan of Charlie Chaplin and *The Kid* fame."

Coogan was back in the United States by May 1944 and was discharged in December 1945. Over the next three decades he developed into a popular choice for character roles in film and television—four episodes of *Perry Mason*, as well as spots on *The Lucy Show, Gunsmoke, Peter Gunn, Hawaii Five-O*, and *The Partridge Family*. For those who have any knowledge or memory of Coogan nowadays, he's Uncle Fester.

During his time in uniform, one must wonder how Coogan felt about his more famous ex-wife. In 1943 Grable was doing a studio photo shoot, and among the shots was her in a one-piece bathing suit and high heels. With her back to the camera and blonde tresses piled atop her head, Betty looks over her right shoulder with a come-hither smile. That shot became the most popular pin-up of the war. That same year Grable married bandleader Harry James.

Coogan doubtless saw Grable's photo adorning offices, tents, hangars, huts, and latrines wherever he went and must have fielded endless (and inappropriate) questions about what it was like to be married to the woman with the "million dollar legs."

Coogan was in poor health in his last years, dying in 1984, having packed a lot of living into his sixty-nine years.

****

English-born Freddie Bartholomew achieved Hollywood stardom playing waifs, orphans, and spoiled rich kids in *David Copperfield* (1935), *Little Lord Fauntleroy* (1936) and *Captains Courageous* (1937). By the time the war came around, Freddie was a gangly teenager, and his star was fading—along with his fortune, as his parents and an aunt went to court in a battle for custody of the $1 million he reportedly earned as a youngster.

On January 13, 1943, the eighteen-year-old joined the United States Army Air Forces, but one year later he was a civilian again, worse for wear from a service-related injury.

"I'm going to try and get well and get back in the Army," Bartholomew told a United Press reporter in a January 13, 1944, article. "If I can't make it, I might go back to pictures."

The article states Freddie suffered a serious back injury in a fall on an obstacle course that kept him in an Army hospital in Amarillo, Texas, for seven months. Bartholomew had joined the USAAF in the hope of becoming a flyer, according to the article.

The story was somewhat different when a chain-smoking Bartholomew was interviewed in 1948 for an article in an Adelaide, Australia, newspaper. Bartholomew, who was down under for a theater engagement, broke his back in a seventeen-foot fall in a Texas airplane hangar where he was working as an aircraft mechanic, according to the article.

Freddie's acting career dwindled away to nothing in the decade after the war. He became extremely successful in advertising.

CHAPTER NINE

B-Actor, Ace Pilot

"Every time they showed a picture aboard the Essex, I was scared to death it would be one of mine."

—Wayne Morris

The Hellcat was a beast worthy of its name, with the power, punch, and protection that endeared it to Navy aviators and struck fear in the hearts of the Japanese pilots who had dominated the skies in the first year of the Pacific war. The Grumman F6F did not have the elegant lines of the Mitsubishi A6M5 Zero-sen—the Hellcat's fuselage was stubby and tapered sharply toward the tail section—but it had about 800 more horsepower than the "Zeke." The Hellcat needed that 2,000-horsepower Pratt & Whitney R-2800 radial engine because its weight was more than twice that of the lightweight Japanese Imperial Navy fighter. Armor plating to protect the pilot and vital components and six .50-caliber machine guns put the pounds on this fat cat, yet it could maneuver with the Zeke (the actual U.S. code name), particularly at high altitudes where the air is thinner. It also had a slight edge in speed over the Zeke and could really pour on the power when needed to get into a fight or out of trouble, with a water-injection booster system.

But like most fighters, the Hellcat's cockpit was a tight squeeze for anyone of more than average height and weight. That had to be the case for Lt. Bert DeWayne Morris, a muscular six-foot, two-inch former fullback at the Los Angeles Junior College. By the time the war started, Morris was several years into his career as Wayne Morris, film star.

Military and flying figured into a few of his early films with Warner Bros., including his debut as the navigator of a flying boat in 1936's *China Clipper* with Pat O'Brien and Humphrey Bogart. A year later, Morris was the titular character in *Kid Galahad*, playing a prize fighter with Warner Bros. royalty Edward G. Robinson, Bette Davis, and Bogart billed above him.

Morris found himself paired up with Bogart a couple more times in *Men are Such Fools* (1938) and a 1939 film Bogart would drink to forget, *The Return of Doctor X*. Morris is top-billed as a reporter looking into a series of mysterious deaths. Bogart plays a resurrected mad scientist who needs human blood to survive. Studio boss Jack Warner was known to punish actors who made salary demands or rejected scripts by casting them in ridiculous roles. Just two years before *The Maltese Falcon*, Bogey looks embarrassed and creepy with pancake makeup, rouge, and a white skunk line through his hair.

Between those two films, Morris had one of his best roles as scheming Virginia Military Institute cadet Billy Randolph in *Brother Rat*. The cast includes a couple of other future World War II veterans, Ronald Reagan and Eddie Albert, along with Regan's first wife, Jane Wyman. Reagan would spend the war fighting the Battle of Culver City for the USAAF, his eyesight apparently too bad to put him in the cockpit of a real airplane. Albert joined the U.S. Coast Guard, then became a U.S. Navy reservist, distinguishing himself in the saving of lives during the invasion of Tarawa in November 1943. The atoll was surrounded by shallow coral reefs, in some places extending hundreds of yards offshore. Landing craft and the marines inside them were stranded in shallow water under heavy enemy fire. Albert piloted a landing craft through several trips rescuing dozens of marines and was awarded a bronze star for his valor that day.

Morris entered into a brief marriage in 1939 with tobacco heiress Leonora Schinasi, divorcing the following year. In 1940, he played second banana to Dennis Morgan in *Flight Angels*, a movie about pilots and stewardesses training for commercial airline service, at which time he decided to earn his pilot's license. Talk about method acting!

The decision to get his wings—and his next marriage—would set the course of his naval career.

Wayne Morris took a break from his Hollywood career to play his greatest role, U.S. Navy ace. Morris earned his wings before the war, after playing the second lead in *Flight Angels*.

Morris joined the Naval Reserve before Pearl Harbor and in 1942 took Patricia Ann O'Rourke as his wife. O'Rourke's uncle was Lieutenant Commander David McCampbell, who would go on to command Air Group 15, the fighter, dive-bomber, and torpedo-bomber squadrons that would serve a memorable deployment on the USS *Essex* in 1944. Morris took advantage of his uncle-in-law not to avoid combat but to ensure he was in the thick of the fighting.

About the time McCampbell was taking command of VF-15 (the fighter squadron for Air Group 15), Morris was a primary flight-training instructor in Hutchinson, Kansas, according to *McCampbell's Heroes* by Edwin P. Hoyt. Morris asked McCampbell to get him into a fighter squadron and McCampbell told him, "Give me a letter."

Morris wrote that letter, but instead of a fighter squadron he found himself transferred to a PBY (patrol-bomber) unit in Jacksonville, Florida. Hoyt wrote that Morris was assigned to Catalina amphibious aircraft because of his size. When he ran into McCampbell in Jacksonville, Morris again asked McCampbell to "get me into fighters."

"McCampbell wanted men who wanted to be fighter pilots more than anything else," Hoyt wrote. Morris got his transfer to VF-15, or "Fighting Fifteen."

For carrier pilots, the danger began months before their first combat sortie. There has never been an aircraft produced in any numbers that did not crash due to pilot error or mechanical failure, and the Hellcat was no exception. Nor was the Helldiver or the Grumman Avenger torpedo plane. In the months of training leading up to deployment on the *Essex*, Air Group 15 lost a dozen pilots and crewman and at least as many planes. Routine military flight training was dangerous under the best of circumstances. When attempting a takeoff or landing from a carrier deck pitching and rolling ten or twenty feet in heavy seas, it could be downright deadly. And the Hellcat pilots were expected to do more than shoot down Betty bombers and mix it up with Zeros, Oscars, Tonys, and Hamps. They were also trained in bombing and strafing sea and land targets.

Lieutenant Morris splashed his first Zero off Guam on June 20, 1944, part of the harvest of Japanese aircraft known to history as the "Great Marianas Turkey Shoot." He got after a Zero that dove out of the clouds to attack Helldivers starting to make their runs. After three passes by Morris, the smoking Zero ploughed into the sea. Morris and two other pilots ganged up on a Japanese patrol plane over Mindanao on September 9, and the next day he led a fighter sweep over two airfields, lighting up camouflaged fuel dumps secreted in a wooded area. He bagged another Zero on September 13. A few days later, he and another pilot rocketed a docked submarine. The Hellcat was a good platform for rockets and five-hundred-pound bombs, and Morris led a fighter sweep over Okinawa on October 10 that sank an eight-thousand-ton freighter. On the same sortie, he shot down a Tony. Two weeks later—October 24—Morris and other Hellcat pilots were trying to pick off Japanese bombers attacking the fleet, and their Zero escorts. He got two Zeros that day, although his F6F took heavy enemy fire—the American emphasis on armor protection for pilots and crew might have saved his life that day.

By the end of his six-month combat tour with the Air Group 15 on *Essex*, the *B* movie actor had become an ace fighter pilot. In fifty-seven missions from a carrier's wood-plank deck, Morris downed seven enemy aircraft—two more than the five needed to become an ace. Lt. B. D. Morris had also taken part in bombing and strafing missions against enemy freighters, destroyers, barges, and that submarine, in addition to strafing aircraft on the ground and destroying other military targets and materiel. An Associated Press brief on his return from the Pacific in December 1944 states that in addition to the seven "Jap Zeros," Morris was credited with "sinking an escort vessel and a flak gunboat and helping sink a submarine and damage a heavy cruiser and a mine layer." Those are fine accomplishments, but hardly rare among the aviators of VF-15. Hoyt lists twenty-six aces among its members: McCampbell was credited with nine kills in one day alone, for which he was later awarded the Congressional Medal of Honor.

Carrier pilot is a high-risk job in peacetime, and in war Morris had his close calls. His IMDb minibio states that three of his aircraft were pushed over the side of *Essex* after missions, considered too damaged to be worth repairing. He was awarded four Distinguished Flying Crosses and two Air Medals.

"As to what a fellow thinks when he's scared, I guess it's the same with anyone," Morris said after the war. "You get fleeting glimpses in your mind of your home, your wife, the baby you want to see." Waxing philosophical, he continued, "You see so clearly the mistakes you made. You want another chance to correct those mistakes. You wonder how you could have attached so much importance to ridiculous, meaningless things in your life. But before you get to thinking too much, you're off into action and everything else is forgotten."

Before the war, Morris appeared in more than two dozen films. He was in another three dozen after the war, including supporting roles in some A-productions. Mostly he was a working actor, lucky enough to be top-billed in some low-budget Westerns and crime dramas, or to lend support to Johnny Sheffield in one of his Bomba movies. His postwar film credits include titles such as *The Bushwhackers*, *Desert Pursuit*, and *Fighting Lawman*. He got to play to type in a supporting role in Gary Cooper's 1949 aircraft-carrier film, *Task Force*.

Did the war keep him from reaching his full potential as an actor? It's impossible to say, although he remained a very busy actor, on the small screen as well as the silver one. The other question is, was he a good actor?

In 1957 Stanley Kubrick cast Morris as Lieutenant Roget in *Paths of Glory*, which ranks with *All Quiet on the Western Front* as the best films about World War I. Roget is a coward who lets soldiers die and passes the blame for his cowardice on to others.

Morris playing a coward? Now that's acting.

The actor/ace died young: he was just forty-five when he suffered a fatal heart attack on September 14, 1959. But his death had a touch of poetry. Morris collapsed on the aircraft carrier *Bon Homme Richard* off the coast of Monterey, California. He was aboard watching air operations with the ship's skipper—and his former commander—Captain David McCampbell.

CHAPTER TEN
The Lone Eagle's Secret War

*Senator Claude Pepper: "Colonel, when did you first go
to Europe?"*

Charles Lindbergh: "Nineteen twenty-seven, sir."

The Japanese land- and carrier-based fighter planes and
bombers enjoyed an advantage over American aircraft
through much of the war: endurance. By designing and building lightweight planes, training pilots to reduce fuel consump-
tion, and developing experience in navigating the vastness of
the Pacific Ocean and its islands, these pilots could strike from
a greater range than their American opponents. Longer range
also bettered the odds that a pilot could avoid ditching and
return safely to his land base or aircraft carrier.

In 1944 a fallen American hero worked with the marine fliers and USAAF to close the gap.

Senator Pepper asked Lindbergh about his travels at the beginning of a Senate hearing in early 1941. Tim Rowland, a columnist for the *Herald-Mail,* wrote in 2019 that the name Lindbergh means as little to most Americans today as that of Hernando de Soto, but when he landed the Spirit of St. Louis at Le Bourget Aerodrome outside Paris on May 21, 1927 (that's right, Senator), he became the greatest celebrity of his age.

As the world had celebrated the first solo nonstop transatlantic flight between New York and Paris, a nation would later grieve with Charles and Anne Morrow Lindbergh when their toddler, Charles Lindbergh Jr., was kidnapped and killed in 1932. The trial and execution of Bruno Richard Hauptmann kept the Lindbergh name before the public into the mid-1930s.

As the specter of war loomed over Europe in the later 1930s, Lindbergh, like millions of other Americans, wanted to keep this country out of the coming conflict. Lindbergh became the most prominent name in the America First Committee, addressing tens of thousands in person and millions over the radio.

Along with isolationists, the America First movement attracted some unsavory characters: profascists, archconservatives, socialists, and anti-Semites. In his speeches and writings, Lindbergh expressed the kind of low-key anti-Semitism that was all too acceptable in polite society of the era. As Lindbergh drew supporters to the movement, he also became a lightning rod for its detractors.

In April 1941, Lindbergh, believing critics were attacking his patriotism, resigned from the Army Air Corps colonelcy bestowed upon him after his historic flight.

In his Pulitzer Prize–winning 1998 biography of the Lone Eagle, *Lindbergh,* A. Scott Berg goes into great detail about his entire life and legacy. In September 1941, days after the invasion of Poland, Lindbergh gave an America First speech in Des Moines, Iowa, that broke the camel's back:

No person with a sense of the dignity of mankind can condone the persecution of the Jewish race in Germany. But no person of honesty and vision can look on their pro-war policy here today without seeing the dangers involved in such a policy, both for us and for them.

That's certainly not as nakedly anti-Jewish as a Louis Farrakhan speech, but it was a bad speech at a worse time. The temperament of the nation was by then decidedly pro-British (Lindbergh blamed them for the war in the same speech), if not as enthusiastic about the plight of European Jews.

After December 7, 1941, Lindbergh was in a sort of limbo: out of the Army with no prospect of being welcomed back, while anxious to do his part in the war. His isolationism disappeared with the Japanese attacks on Pearl Harbor and the Philippines.

Roosevelt and others did not want Lindbergh to have any visible role in the war effort, but Lindbergh was an intuitive pilot and engineer whose interests extended to medical technology and other fields. Berg notes Lindbergh's prewar work in the development of what would later evolve into the heart-lung machine. But the onetime "most famous man on Earth" had achieved pariah status—no major arms manufacturer wanted to offend the Roosevelt administration or garner the bad publicity of putting on the payroll a man who received an honorary decoration from Luftwaffe Chief Herman Goering just a few years earlier. (Lindbergh had been similarly honored by many nations, and Goering did not personally present the award.)

Lindbergh landed a position with the Ford Motor Company. It would be too easy to note that the doddering founder of the company was America's best known anti-Semite, Henry Ford. Lindbergh, despite being well into middle age by standards of the day, became a guinea pig for high-altitude testing, nearly losing his life when a faulty gauge led to him running out of oxygen seven miles high in a P-47 Thunderbolt.

Being a test pilot did not satisfy a man who, by his very nature, sought out challenges. He wrangled an assignment as a "technician" in the Pacific, albeit one who arrived in theater in Brooks Brother fatigues. He was greeted with some suspicion before establishing himself as the legendary flier he still was. A decade or two older than most pilots, he flew marine F4U Corsairs and USAAF P-38 Lightnings on bombing and strafing missions.

"If there is life wherever that bomb hit, you have taken it," he wrote after one mission. Lindbergh went from one jungle airbase to another, instructing aviators on how to stretch their mileage. He taught pilots to raise manifold pressure and lower RPMs. Some pilots resisted, but those who followed

Lindbergh's methods saw the range and endurance of their aircraft increase by two hours and two hundred miles.

With a wink and a nudge from superiors all the way up to General Douglas MacArthur, Lindbergh got the okay to keep flying combat missions, still officially as a civilian observer. On July 28, 1944, piloting a P-38 he got into an aerial scrum, firing his .50-caliber machine guns in a head-on duel with an overmatched Sonia dive bomber, which he splashed.

Lindbergh continued on in his observer and technician roles, completing fifty missions without once donning his country's uniform.

Despite his earlier desire for America to stay out of what he felt was a European war, Lindbergh jumped in with both feet once the United States was attacked. But time did not change his opinion that the war was, on balance, a loss for the country and the world as a whole. He wrote the following in a letter to the publisher of his journals more than two decades later:

> We won the war in a military sense; but in a broader sense it seems to me we lost it, for our Western civilization is less respected and secure than it was before.
>
> In order to defeat Germany and Japan we supported the still greater menaces of Russia and China—which now confront us in a nuclear weapon era. The British empire has broken down with great suffering, bloodshed and confusion. France has had to give up her major colonies and turn to a mild dictatorship herself.

Lindbergh continued that the war resulted in the strengthening of the Soviet Union, which "dropped their Iron Curtain to screen off Eastern Europe," while Communist China posed a great threat to U.S. interests in Asia. The war did not make the world safe for democracy, as the American military stationed forces in Europe and Asia to hold off the communist threat in two hemispheres.

"It is alarmingly possible that World War II marks the beginning of our Western civilization's breakdown," the aging aviator wrote.

Lindbergh's view of the postwar world had some legitimacy: Once-democratic nations in Eastern Europe spent decades under Soviet domination; the Chinese traded a generalissimo for a chairman; and communism became entrenched in North Korea and, later, Cuba. After the fall of the Soviet Union, Russia had a brief affair with democracy before reverting to the comfortable familiarity of dictatorship under Vladimir Putin.

On the other side of the ledger, Lindbergh did not live to see a unified and democratic Germany or the nations of Eastern Europe regain their independence. Lindbergh could not have failed to see that Japan became a Westernized democracy within a remarkably short time after the war, while the Asian, African, and Middle Eastern colonies European countries had to surrender after the war became independent nations, with some achieving great prosperity.

Contrary to the gloomy future Lindbergh envisioned in his final years, much of the world has benefited by adopting Western values, not dismantling them.

CHAPTER ELEVEN
Kolberg

Nettlebeck: "We'd rather be buried under the rubble than surrender."

Gneisenau: "That's what I wanted to hear. Now we can die together!"

That bit of Gotterdammerung dialogue was almost certainly penned by Nazi Propaganda Minister Joseph Goebbels, one of the screenwriters, though uncredited, for *Kolberg*. This big-budget patriotic epic cost millions of Reichsmarks, was more than two years in the making, featured a cast of thousands, and premiered just in time to provide some inspiration to the beleaguered German people before the complete and utter collapse of the Third Reich.

The movie, filmed in glorious Agfacolor, premiered in Berlin on January 30, 1945, the twelfth and last anniversary of Adolf Hitler being named chancellor of Germany. Had Goebbels waited to premiere *Kolberg* for Hitler's birthday on April 20, the movie could have been projected onto a white bedsheet hung from a dank concrete wall of the *Führerbunker*. As it was, the number of functioning movie houses in Germany was dwindling fast, and food and survival were higher priorities than date-night entertainment for the citizens of the crumbling Reich. Instead of boosting the national spirit and extending Germany's lost cause, the resources devoted to making *Kolberg* might actually have helped shorten the war and save a few lives on all sides.

When one thinks of Nazi cinema—if one does at all—what comes most often to mind are *Triumph of the Will* and *Olympia*, both prewar works of director Leni Riefenstahl. Even with her poor choice of political loyalties, Riefenstahl was recognized as a pioneer among documentarians, male or female, and she earned the pariah status that followed her after the war. Over the past eighty or so years, those films are more talked and written about than seen. Despite some remarkable imagery in *Triumph of the Will* and *Olympia*, pacing was not Riefenstahl's forte. Both films are boring.

Triumph of the Will (1935) is a propaganda piece chronicling the annual Nazi Party rally at Nuremburg, a city better known to history for the war crimes trials and executions of 1946. *Olympia*, a two-part film running nearly four hours in total, is a documentary of the 1936 Berlin Olympics. There is plenty of adoring slow-motion footage of Aryan cheesecake and beefcake on display, but Riefenstahl also features the star of the games, American track and field champion Jesse Owens, a departure from the Third Reich's racialist policies. Despite beautiful black-and-white cinematography and somewhat less overt propaganda than *Triumph of the Will*, it is a slog getting through *Olympia*, even in two sittings.

Through the early decades of the twentieth century, Germany was on the cutting edge of the movie business. Crack open just about any book on the history of cinema and *The Cabinet of Dr. Caligari*, *Nosferatu*, *Metropolis*, *The Blue Angel*, and *M* will be analyzed, essayed, and praised in print. Most of those classics are better read about than watched. (Okay, *M* is pretty good, thanks to Peter Lorre.) When the Nazi Party came to power, much of the movie talent in Germany, and later in greater Europe, relocated to the welcoming environment and sunnier climate of Southern California. The growing anti-Semitism in Europe during the 1930s and the vastly greater opportunities in Hollywood made emigrating an easy decision for many Jews in the industry, much to Hollywood's benefit. Gentiles frightened of, or repulsed by, the fascists also sought work in Hollywood: Conrad Veidt and Marlene Dietrich, to name two.

Once the war got under way, the Nazi film industry continued to crank out romances, comedies, musicals, melodramas, and other escapist fare to keep the people's and soldiers' minds off the unpleasantries of North Africa, Stalingrad, the strategic bombing campaign, D-Day, and the other self-inflicted disasters that befell Germany.

Joseph Goebbels green-lit *Kolberg* in 1942, perhaps figuring the *Herrenvolk* needed a pick-me-up as the tide of the war turned against the Axis. The story was an inspiring one:

In 1806 the citizens of Kolberg defended their city against Napoleon's forces until the siege was finally broken. It was also as historically inaccurate as any American "historical" movie. Being a period piece and a war movie, *Kolberg* needed a lot of extras to portray soldiers and civilians in Napoleonic-era uniforms and period costumes, antique cannons and muskets, horses for the cavalry charges, and indoor and outdoor sets.

Veteran director of Jew-bashing movies, Veit Harlan, got the nod to helm *Kolberg*, and his wife, Kristina Söderbaum was cast as the female lead. Filming took about ten months, wrapping up in August 1944—about the time the Western Allies were liberating Paris. Produced by UFA, the film's final cut was finished at its studio in Potsdam—Stalin, Churchill, and Harry Truman would be holding a Big Three pow-wow there in July 1945. Agfacolor, Germany's answer to Technicolor, is comparable in the richness of its hues and the cinematography is first class.

In the film world of Nazi German propaganda Viet Harlan and Kristina Söderbaum were a power couple, with Söderbaum starring in more than a dozen films her husband directed, including several made after the war. Their wartime work included *Jud Suss* in 1940 and *Die goldene Stadt* (*The Golden City*) in 1942. In both films Söderbaum suffers that "fate worse than death," in the former at the hands of Joseph Suss Oppenheimer, a real-life eighteenth-century Jewish advisor to the Duke of Württemberg. In *The Golden City* Söderbaum is Anna, a Sudeten German girl seduced by a Czech. Having been defiled by a Jew in the one film and a non-Germanic Czech in the other, Söderbaum's characters end their shame by drowning themselves. Söderbaum's character suffers a near-drowning at the hands of her husband, who is having an affair with a foreign woman, in *The Trip to Tilsit* from 1939. This recurring denouement led to her being dubbed the "Riechswasserleiche," which translates (poorly) to "The Reich's Water Corpse."

Söderbaum became the personification of the ideal German Frau or Fräulein, a fair-skinned, blue-eyed blonde "who is frequently identified as the National Socialist star who most closely approximated the Nazi ideal of womanhood," according to *Hitler's Heroines: Stardom and Womanhood in Nazi Cinema*, by Antje Ascheid. However, this Aryan ideal of womanhood was not even German: Söderbaum was born in Sweden. She was an attractive, healthy, and wholesome-looking woman, though her features appear a bit severe at some angles. Men no doubt found her alluring in a Donna Reed (apologies to the late Ms. Reed) sort of way: sexy without being overtly sexual. Women might have seen Söderbaum's screen image as something to aspire to, rather than to be threatened by.

Strange claims have been made about *Kolberg*; the most preposterous was that more than 180,000 soldiers were used in the production. Ascheid puts the number at a far more realistic five thousand. As bad as the war was going for Germany, not even a couple of masterminds like Hitler and Goebbels would have withdrawn the equivalent of ten full-strength divisions from the fronts or from other more important duties. No single shot in the movie—of citizens marching in the streets or digging moats, cavalry or infantry charges, artillery barrages—would appear to have much more than a thousand or so people in the frame at any one time.

The budget was about 8 million Reichsmarks, which might have made it among the most expensive movies up to that time, but the value of wartime currency (especially for a losing country) is difficult to calculate. In 1940 $1 was worth about RM 2.5, and, the following year, the United States and Germany quit doing business. *Gone with the Wind* cost about $4 million by the time it hit the big screen in 1939. Both the United States dollar and German currency (Germany changed over to the Euro in 2002) saw their values inflated many times over the decades, so a dollar-Reichsmark comparison is further complicated. Whatever amount of money was spent to make *Kolberg*, it was not being used to manufacture ammunition, Me 262 jet fighters, or King Tiger tanks.

Though filmed over a period that included the winter of 1943–44, one hundred railcars filled with salt were brought in to simulate snow in scenes filmed during warmer weather. This may have been a matter of having better control over filming conditions by using fake snow instead of trusting Mother Nature to provide some on schedule. That was one hundred railcars not being used to haul Jewish prisoners to concentration camps for a time or to take munitions, rations, and other supplies to the front. The film has a lot of horses, which meant that during filming they were not hauling artillery pieces, soldiers, food, and ordnance. German infantry divisions required thousands of horses to move—trucks were a luxury used to support panzer and panzergrenadier divisions.

Presumably the German movie industry had plenty of period costumes and uniforms in storage—or maybe they didn't. Making all that apparel meant materials and labor were being diverted from the production of uniforms, boots, and tents. Every tradesman building a set was one not using his talents to aid the war effort.

For all the resources it consumed, *Kolberg* runs less than two hours. It is a well-made, stylish, and action-filled piece of cinema, if one ignores the rousing (or shrill) speeches that break out from time to time. There is an impressive tracking shot in one cavalry charge, and the battle scenes are well produced, though somewhat bloodless. One extra played his death scene just the way a Hollywood extra would in the 1940s: clutch chest, grimace, spin a half turn, and keel over.

Kolberg premiered at a temporary outdoor cinema in Berlin at the end of January. A copy was also parachuted to soldiers in La Rochelle, a naval base the Allies chose to bypass and let wither on the vine rather than spend lives taking. Three months later, Hitler would shoot himself in his bunker, and, on May 8, 1945, Germany surrendered, and the movie ended its run. During this time, the city of Kolberg was placed under siege by the Red Army. There was no happy ending for the city's defenders.

Having been crucial cogs in the creative team behind several racialist and anti-Semitic films, movies of which Goebbels and his henchmen controlled the budgets and content, it is a surprise that Harlan and Söderbaum remained together and continued making movies after the war. Harlan, prosecuted but acquitted on charges of crimes against humanity for his wartime films, directed seven more films between 1950 and 1958, dying in 1964. One of his last was *The Third Sex* (also known as *Bewildered* Youth), a melodrama about parents concerned their son is being lured into a homosexual lifestyle.

Söderbaum, who died in 2001, continued to appear in films into 1993.

Here are two odd postscripts on Harlan, a man synonymous with anti-Semitic propaganda films: he was briefly married in the 1920s to Dora Gerson, a Jewish actress and singer who would perish two decades later in Auschwitz, and Harlan's niece Christiane Harlan married American director Stanley Kubrick, who happened to be Jewish.

Under her stage name Susanne Christian, Christiane Harlan played the German girl forced to sing for the French soldiers at the very end of Kubrick's great World War I movie, *Paths of Glory*.

CHAPTER TWELVE
Slaughter on a Smaller Scale

> *"War, conflict. It's all business. One murder makes a villain. Millions a hero."*
>
> —Charlie Chaplin in *Monsieur Verdoux*

The Nazis had tens of thousands of willing accomplices and coerced abettors in their murder of six million Jews and millions of other so-called *Untermenschen*.

Dr. Marcel Petiot preferred to work alone. Petiot scammed dozens of people desperate to leave Europe into paying him thousands of francs in exchange for passage via the underground to Portugal and on to South America. None of them made it further than the Seine River. Others did not get out of his basement. In his early days as a serial killer, Petiot employed a few henchmen in the disposal of body parts, but his greed and lack of trust were such that he did not bring any full partners into his scheme.

A one-time soldier, black marketeer (particularly of French Army supplies), physician, and mayor of Villeneuve, Petiot somehow managed to get a medical license and, as war and the collapse of the Third Republic approached, hung his shingle at two addresses in Paris. As the Wehrmacht overran France, there was no shortage of people with good reason to get out of France, making the City of Lights a target-rich environment for his murderous schemes.

When Petiot began murdering people is in question. Rumors surrounded the disappearance of a young servant girl with whom he was involved when he was practicing medicine and skimming from the public trough as mayor of Villeneuve. His work certainly began in earnest after the fall of France as body parts began turning up in the river. As a physician, Petiot had access to medicines and poisons and used his license as a way of eliminating clients without having delivered his promised service of safe passage. Using the ruse of administering inoculations against typhoid or other diseases, the bad doctor was instead injecting them with cyanide or strychnine.

As it became riskier to dump the dead in the river, Petiot instead turned to a method that the Nazi regime was using in its extermination camps—incineration. It was also how an earlier serial killer from an earlier war tried to eradicate the evidence of his crimes. Henri Landru, the French Bluebeard, was in the 1910s another swindler who prospered during wartime, although his modus operandi was different in that he sought his victims from another demographic. During the Great War, France saw the flower of its manhood disappear in the muddy trenches and no-man's-land of the Western Front. Many of those French soldiers left behind wives and children ripe to be exploited by a man offering companionship and matrimony.

A married father of four, Landru operated out of a villa in Gambais during the war years, but it was not until a year after the war ended that inquiries to the mayor from the relatives of missing women finally prompted action. Landru, who lived under an assumed name in the city, had by then moved, but an examination of the villa's stove turned up hundreds of bone and tooth fragments, as well as clothing and possessions of victims. Landru was tried and convicted in 1921 and lost his head the following year.

As with Landru, it was the cremation of his victims that was the beginning of the end for Petiot. On March 11, 1944, there was a chimney fire at his Paris residence while the doctor was out. Firemen and gendarmes responded, forcing their way inside to put out the fire and finding a house of horrors in the process. Hunks of burning human remains were found in a furnace, as well as body parts set aside for later incineration, enough to assemble into ten bodies. This naturally led to some questions from the police about what Petiot was up to. When confronted, the doctor was quick on his feet, claiming he was disposing of the bodies of collaborators and informers assassinated by the Resistance. It must have been Inspector Clouseau who was assigned to the case, because Petiot was not immediately arrested; he made use of this lucky break to absent himself from Paris.

In addition to body parts, gendarmes found dozens of suitcases, as well as piles of clothing and other belongings of men, women, and children. Investigators would later charge that Petiot would even go to the homes of his victims after he had dispatched them, to steal whatever other valuables they left behind.

Ironically, the pretend patriot of the Resistance joined the Free French Army. Instead of lying low under his nom de guerre, Petiot decided he needed to defend his reputation and declare his innocence in print, penning letters to a magazine, *Resistance*, under the alias, "Captain Henri Valery," according to *The New Encyclopedia of Serial Killers* by Brian Lane and Wilfred Gregg. Having been a physician and public official, Petiot left behind plenty of exemplars of his handwriting. Investigators were able to compare those to the letters posted by the magazine. They were able to put *deux et deux* together and it came out *quatre*. Petiot was arrested and stood trial for the murders. The doctor continued to assert that he acted in league with Resistance groups but could not provide any proof. Petiot was convicted of twenty-seven counts of murder, though he claimed to have killed up to sixty-three—all for the glory of France.

Whatever the actual number, the punishment would have been the same. Like Landru, Petiot went under the blade of the guillotine on May 26, 1946.

****

Whatever demons drove Petiot, profit was certainly one of them. Most serial killers are motivated by lust, sadism, or a combination of the two. Bruno Lüdke would have fit that profile, though he might not have fit the crimes German police pinned on him.

There is no stereotypical lust-driven serial killer; serial killers range from the outwardly charming necrophiliac Theodore Bundy to psychotics such as the "Vampire of Sacramento," Richard Chase. The former could easily move about society without raising suspicions, while the latter was so mentally disturbed he could not step outside his home without drawing bewildered and frightened stares.

Born in 1908 or 1909 in Köpenick, Germany, Bruno Lüdke was mentally challenged from his youth but able to secure employment driving delivery trucks and horse carts. He also performed pickup and delivery for his family's laundry business. During the late 1930s, Lüdke was given a sort of "intelligence test" by police after people complained of how cruelly he treated his horse. Lüdke was unable to say how many days there are in a year, but he got the name of the Reich chancellor correct: Adolf Hitler.

Lüdke established himself as a sexual criminal when he was arrested for rape in the late 1930s. Found mentally defective, Lüdke was not tried for the crime but was instead sterilized, a not-uncommon practice during the Nazi regime for those with mental or physical defects. For some reason, Lüdke was later released back into the community.

His sterilization did not stop Lüdke from murdering and sexually assaulting women, if German authorities are to be believed. On January 29, 1943, fifty-one-year-old Frieda Rössner was found strangled in a wooded area outside Berlin. Lüdke lived nearby and supposedly knew the victim as a customer of the family laundry. When questioned by police, he went berserk, attacking his interrogators before being subdued.

Lüdke, still immune from prosecution under German law, confessed to Rössner's murder and scores of others, a death toll he began ringing up in 1928. Torturing or influencing a deranged or intellectually-challenged suspect into confessions—true or false—might have been standard procedure and easy work for German police of the day. Lüdke was institutionalized in a hospital for the criminally insane but might have wished for a trial and execution if he knew what was in store. Though he could not be tried, he could be used as a human guinea pig for Nazi medical research. It was in a Vienna hospital that an injection that was part of one such experiment proved fatal. Thus he met the same fate as the concentration camp prisoners the Nazis used for medical "research."

Questions have been raised about whether Lüdke was a fall guy for police, who were able to close the books on fifty or more sex murders thanks to the perhaps coerced confessions of a mental defective. More than seven decades later, it is difficult to judge the forensic capabilities of German police during wartime. Lüdke's story cannot be easily wrapped up like an episode of *CSI: Berlin*. However, Lüdke had a long record of mostly minor crimes and a reputation for cruelty to animals. Further, he had been accused in an earlier sexual crime, and his job as a deliveryman allowed him to go from place to place where he could find the targets of his lust without drawing untoward attention.

****

There was no doubt on the guilt of Gordon Frederick Cummins, the "Blackout Ripper" of World War II London. Cummins, who killed and mutilated four women in a matter of five days in 1942, was more a spree killer than a serial killer in that, although he had the requisite number of three murders to achieve serial-killer status, there wasn't much of a cooling-off period between kills.

The twenty-five-year-old RAF cadet strangled Evelyn Hamilton in an air raid shelter on February 9, 1942, and showgirl Evelyn Oatley in her London flat the next night. Oatley had been mutilated with a can-opener. Margaret Lowe was found strangled with silk stockings in her apartment on February 13, with the body of Doris Jouannet being found just hours later. Cummins attacked two other women that night. He was scared off when a passerby interrupted his assault on a woman in a shop doorway, while another victim broke free of him and screamed her lungs out to alert the neighborhood.

In the first of those two nonfatal assaults, Cummins left behind the clue that would send him to the gallows: his RAF-issued gas mask. By its serial number, police linked it to the airman it had been issued to, Gordon Cummins. His arrest also provided investigators with his fingerprints, which were matched to prints found at some of the murder scenes and the tin opener used to mutilate Oatley.

At the end of a one-day trial, the jury deliberated thirty-five minutes before finding Cummins guilty of the Oatley murder. Cummins met the famous English hangman Albert Pierrepoint at Wandsworth Prison on June 25, 1942.

****

A few months after Cummins committed his crimes, and half-way around the world in Melbourne, Australia, three women were throttled to death in quick succession by a man who came to be dubbed the "Brownout Strangler." The nickname came from the fact that Australians were not as stringent as Londoners when it came to nighttime lighting restrictions.

Between May 3 and 18, 1942, the bodies of three women were found in Melbourne: forty-year-old Ivy McLeod, thirty-one-year-old Pauline Thompson, and forty-year-old Gladys Hosking. McLeod and Thompson had their clothing nearly torn from their body, but neither appeared to have been, as one newspaper delicately called it, "criminally assaulted." All were found outdoors, and each had been beaten and strangled, though the doctor who performed the autopsy on Thompson described her death as being unusual in method.

"It was not strangulation in the ordinary sense," Dr. Crawford Henry Mollison testified at one proceeding. "It was due to pressure on the nerves of the neck causing paralysis of the heart."

"A small, hand-picked force of detectives has been assigned to special brown-out duty, following a second mystery murder in the last week," the *Courier-Mail* of Brisbane reported after the murders of McLeod and Thompson. "They have been given a roving commission in the city, but will operate chiefly in areas where large numbers of girls are employed on night shifts at munitions factories. Detectives believe that a maniac killer is at large."

The perpetrator was in custody within days of the Hosking murder. Melbourne was crawling with American GIs from Camp Pell. Pauline Thompson, a constable's wife, had been seen the night of her demise in the company of a U.S. soldier. Other women reported being threatened or accosted by a soldier of a similar description, and an Australian soldier provided what one newspaper called a valuable clue—likely a description of a disheveled GI shortly after the Hosking murder. Investigators soon focused on a clearly nuts twenty-four-year-old private by the name of Edward Joseph Leonski.

The innocent and boyish grin of Private First Class Eddie Leonski conceals the darker side of the "Brownout Strangler." The serial killer strangled three women in Melbourne, Australia, in 1942. He wanted their voices.

Leonski was on a crawl through Melbourne's bars and drinking many pints of beer before staggering down the city's darkened streets in search of the companionship of the local gals—in the case of the victims, considerably older gals. His army photo showed a young man with a boyish face and a wide, toothy smile. The happy-go-lucky face beaming from the front pages of Austrailian dailies—he had a smile like Potsie from *Happy Days*—gave no hint of any mental illness. Leonski would be examined by psychiatrists in June, a month before his court-martial.

"Leonski did not give evidence on his own behalf, but evidence for the defense was called to show the peculiarities of the accused when he was under the influence of alcohol, and that he was not responsible for his actions," read one newspaper account of his court-martial. The defense also presented evidence of mental illness within Leonski's immediate family. One psychiatrist for the judge advocate testified Leonski had "a psychopathic personality with psychosis," but that did not mean he was legally insane.

He certainly exhibited odd behavior, with one newspaper article referring to evidence at his trial that "Leonski was seen to mix beer, ice cream, whisky, ketchup, and hot peppers and drink the concoction." Nowadays you can probably find dare-takers on YouTube pulling similar stunts while drunk, but Eddie did have one brother who had earlier been committed to an asylum, and his own behavior in uniform—fueled by alcohol—had become increasingly chaotic.

Even for a spree or serial killer, the circumstances of Leonski's murders are almost pedestrian—drunken soldier beats and strangles trio of females. Yet his confessed motive exhibits the peculiarity of an unbalanced mind:

"It was to get their voices," Eddie told investigators. As he walked Pauline Thompson home, she sang for him, and "I could feel myself going mad about it. . . . She had a lovely voice. I wanted that voice. I grabbed her around the neck. . . . I choked her. I choked her," he said of one victim.

"She was singing in my ear and looking in my eyes," Leonski said of another. "I grabbed her and told her to keep on singing. . . . I choked her."

Perhaps it was a story he concocted to buttress his attorney's assertion that Leonski was mad as a hatter. Just maybe he was mad as a hatter. Either way, the "Brownout Strangler" picked up another nickname: the "Singing Strangler."

The general court-martial ended with Leonski being found guilty of the murders and condemned to the gallows. On November 9, 1942, Leonski was reportedly heard singing softly in his cell hours before he was hanged.

CHAPTER THIRTEEN

Taiho

"I don't have the altitude, Mike. We'll take this ride together."

—Ens. Hans Jacobson from *Wing and a Prayer*

Ronald Reagan could tell a tale and, at his best, hold an audience in the palm of his hand, his Pointe du Hoc speech at the fortieth anniversary of D-Day being a prime example of his relating a true story with an actor's skill. The fortieth president could also spin an anecdote with a bit of fact, a movie line, and a wisp of thin air, then pass it off as the truth. That is not to say such stories were out-and-out lies, as Reagan likely believed what he was telling an audience to be the truth. How many of us have heard a story, convincingly told, and believed it to be a fact? How many of us have then told that tale to someone else?

Reagan's forays into fantasyland could be painfully easy to expose, as the time he told Israeli Prime Minister Yitzhak Shamir about his filming documentary footage at Dachau after the concentration camp was liberated. Reagan was in the U.S. Army Air Force during the war but spent it making training films in Culver City, California. He likely reviewed a lot of the footage within a short time of it being filmed, but watching a movie of an event is a far cry from being there.

In 1983, the president addressed an audience of recipients of the Congressional Medal of Honor, telling them the story of a belly gunner trapped in the ball turret of a battle-damaged B-17 heading for a crash landing as it struggled back to England from a bomb run over Europe. Reagan recounted how the crew could not free the wounded gunner from the turret—a death sentence for him if the plane crashed or made a wheels-up landing. The commander ordered the crew to bail out, but as the last man was about to leave the doomed aircraft, he looked back to see the commander sit down, reach in to the turret to grasp the gunner's hand and say, "Never mind son, we'll ride it down together." Almost as an afterthought, Reagan added, "Congressional Medal of Honor, posthumously awarded."

As the reader has likely gathered by now, no such incident ever happened. Reagan reportedly used the story a number of times during the 1980 presidential campaign, but one writer took a deep dive into Medal of Honor records from the war after that 1983 speech and could find no citation remotely similar to the president's recollection. Were it an outright lie, telling such a story before a room filled with real heroes would make it all the more brazen on Reagan's part.

This piece of fiction appears to have several fathers, beginning with the 1944 20th Century Fox war film *Wing and a Prayer* starring Don Ameche and Dana Andrews. In one scene crew members of Carrier X listen to a conversation between Ens. Hans Jacobson and his injured rear gunner, Mike. Their battle-damaged aircraft is struggling to maintain altitude and return to the carrier, but it is a losing battle. Their final words over the plane's intercom system are somehow piped with crystal clarity across the carrier's public address system:

Mike: "We're burning back here. You'd better bail out, sir."

Jacobson: "I haven't got the altitude, Mike. We'll take this ride together."

Jacobson's dialogue is pretty close to the punchline of Reagan's story. Writer Alec Nevala-Lee noted the similarity in a 2017 article, along with "a similar apocryphal item that appeared that year in *Reader's Digest*." Nevala-Lee went on to note that the story of a trapped belly gunner was used in a 1985 episode of Stephen Spielberg's short-lived NBC series *Amazing Stories*.

Kevin Costner and Kiefer Sutherland were on their way up the celebrity ladder when they appeared in the episode "The Mission." Once again, a gunner is trapped in the belly turret of a shot-up bomber, and the crew cannot lower the landing gear. Thanks to the power of positive thinking by the gunner, the plane sprouts cartoon landing gear with huge balloon tires.

So both Reagan and Spielberg had somehow been exposed to the tale of the trapped gunner, adding their own touches.

Late *60 Minutes* curmudgeon Andy Rooney was a reporter for *Stars and Stripes* during the war and witnessed what might have been the genesis of what became the trapped-gunner story. In his memoir *My War*, Rooney described the 1944 death of a gunner trapped in the jammed ball turret of a crippled B-17 returning to base from a bomb run over heavily defended Regensburg. The man was crushed to death when the bomber was forced to make a wheels-up emergency landing.

"We all watched in horror as it happened," Rooney wrote. "We watched as the man's life ended, mashed between the concrete of the runway and the belly of the bomber."

"During the two years I covered the air war, there were half a dozen stories I couldn't bring myself to write," Rooney wrote, "even if it had been more honest if I had."

The website Snopes.com, which delves into the fact or fiction behind such stories, theorized "an embellishment of an actual incident" Rooney witnessed morphed into the story told by Reagan and filmed by Spielberg. Rooney's book was published years after Reagan's speeches, and the *Amazing Stories* episode, but Rooney doubtless told it to innumerable people in the decades after the war.

However, thousands of USAAF bombers were shot down and shot up during the war. It is possible that another similar tragedy occurred that was not witnessed by Rooney but was seen by airmen who then passed their recollections on.

There is another scene from *Wing and a Prayer* worth mentioning, not as an example of how life imitates art, but as an instance of how art can unintentionally imitate life. During the secret mission of Carrier X, Ensign Charles Cunningham is having a hard time of it, splashing an aircraft in a botched takeoff. Cunningham later redeems himself in an act of self-sacrifice when, seeing the wake of a Japanese torpedo heading toward the carrier, he dives his aircraft into the ocean, intercepting and exploding it in the nick of time.

Wing and a Prayer was released in July 1944 and was no doubt in the final stages of postproduction when the Battle of the Philippine Sea took place in June. The two-day battle was also known as the "Marianas Turkey Shoot," as the Japanese lost approximately six hundred aircraft and three fleet carriers, for the loss of 123 U.S. Navy aircraft. Despite their own losses of aircraft, the Americans were able to save many of the pilots and crew forced to ditch damaged and fuel-starved planes. And planes were easier to replace than trained pilots and crew.

The battle was the first for the Japanese Imperial Navy's newest and most advanced carrier, *Taiho*. Commissioned just three months earlier, the thirty-thousand-ton, 855-foot *Taiho* featured an armored deck and a thicker torpedo belt than its predecessors. *Taiho* ("great phoenix") served as the flagship for Vice-Admiral Jisaburo Ozawa as the Japanese fleet steamed out to meet the U.S. Fifth Fleet. On the morning of the battle's first day, June 19, *Taiho* turned its bow into the wind and began launching a strike package of sixteen Zero fighters, seventeen Judy dive bombers, and nine Jill bombers. Lurking just below the waves was the submarine USS *Albacore*, which launched a spread of six torpedoes at the huge carrier.

Warrant Officer Sakio Komatsu was orbiting *Taiho* when he spotted the wake of at least one of the torpedoes. Acting like the hero of an American war movie, Komatsu broke formation, diving his Judy into the sea and exploding the torpedo in an utterly altruistic act meant to save the 2,150 sailors of his ship—most of whom would be dead by the afternoon despite his heroism. While Komatsu destroyed the one torpedo and four others failed to hit home, the sixth ran true, finding its mark at 7:45 a.m.

The torpedo struck *Taiho's* starboard side near the forward elevator. Damage control crews made sufficient repairs to allow the carrier to begin launching planes within two hours after the explosion, and the ship barely lost a knot of speed.

Taiho's wound was not necessarily mortal, but a ticking time bomb below decks was not properly dealt with by damage-control crews. The explosion fractured fuel oil and aviation gas tanks in the ship's bowels, and, although there was no fire, deadly fumes collected in the hangar deck and below. Similar to British carriers, *Taiho* had an enclosed hangar deck, and a mechanical ventilation system was used in an attempt to disburse the fumes. Still the explosive vapors accumulated below decks and opening more hatches and the aft elevator only served to spread the fumes further and expose them to more possible sources of ignition. Six hours after the torpedo found its mark, a spark or flame set off a fuel-air bomb inside the ship's hull. The resulting explosion ripped through Taiho's innards, incinerating hundreds of crew and rupturing steel plates. Nothing could save the flaming wreck. Ozawa had to be persuaded not to sacrifice his own life and transfer his flag to the cruiser *Haguro*. The admiral survived, but the Great Phoenix rolled over and sank that afternoon, taking more than 1,600 of her sailors to a watery grave.

As the tide of the war in the Pacific turned against Japan, a fatalistic farewell spread among the soldiers, sailors, and airmen. "See you at Yasukuni," they would say when heading out on missions or attacks that were more and more likely to be their last. The Imperial Shrine of Yasukuni is the memorial to

Japanese war dead. Perhaps Sakio Komatsu uttered that somber leave-taking to a fellow pilot or crewman before throttling up the Judy's 1,400-horsepower engine and lifting off into the morning sky.

The makers of *Wing and a Prayer* likely did not know that the concocted derring-do of a script writer's imagination was played out in real life by an enemy pilot just weeks before their film hit theaters.

CHAPTER FOURTEEN
One Unlucky Schlitt

"That's about as funny as a screen door on a battleship."
—Biff Tannen, *Back to the Future*

"It's a screen door on a submarine, you dork."
—Marty McFly

There was precious little to laugh about in a World War II submarine, especially for crews of the *Unterseeboots* of Germany's navy (the Kriegsmarine) from mid-1943 to 1945, as the U.S. and British navies gained the upper hand through a combination of tactics, technology, and weight of numbers. Within the 220-foot length of a Type VIIC U-boat, fifty or more officers and crew had to share space with torpedoes, ammunition, food, and other stores so they could eat and fight for weeks on patrols covering the North Atlantic to the tropics. On many days it was a battle against tedium and a test of tolerance, discipline, and camaraderie as the smell of diesel mixed with belches, farts, sweat, and spoiling food added their fetid odors to the stale air.

The "happy times," as German submariners would later refer to the war's early years, nearly choked off Great Britain's lifeline with the United States but gave way to the slaughter of submariners in the war's final two years. The mid-Atlantic gap, the stretch of ocean where long-range bombers from America and Britain could not patrol, was closed as escort carriers began accompanying convoys. Airborne radar sets in the land-based aircraft improved to the point of being able to pick out a periscope or snorkel poking above the waves. The frigates and destroyers protecting those convoys were equipped with ASDIC and other sonar to improve detection of U-boats. Depth charges and "hedgehogs" breached their pressure hulls, the later by firing a salvo of explosive projectiles in a pattern that upped the chances of a direct and fatal hit.

The wolfpacks went from being the hunters during the happy times to being the hunted. Few sailors survived an attack that claimed their boats. An imploding hull a hundred feet or more below the surface left no chance for survival. In a few cases, damaged subs were able to surface, allowing some fortunate crewmen to scramble out of the hatches and into the sea before these iron coffins made their death plunge. At the right time of the year, at the right latitude, and with the right weather, they might be rescued before they froze to death or drowned. Only the submariners who survived such attacks could even begin to describe the terror.

On May 9, 1941, the Brits were able to use a corvette (a small warship) and destroyers to drop depth charges at a U-boat, U-110, to force it to the surface to be captured. The Royal Canadian Navy and U.S. Navy captured U-boats in 1944.

Life beneath the waves for a submariner from any navy presented challenges that few tourists on a Carnival cruise would recognize. When a child meets an astronaut, the question that often comes to their minds is "How do you go to the bathroom in space?" Using the toilet, or head, of a submarine deep beneath the waves during World War II would be an alien experience for any landlubber and resulted in at least one ship being lost.

Consider the disposal of human waste in the U.S. Navy's "Silent Service." The heads on a Gato-class sub were a maze of pipes, valves, knobs, and levers connected to a small bowl in a space barely large enough to accommodate a man. Read the directions carefully:

Directions for operating

Before using see that bowl flapper valve "a" is closed. Gate valve "c" in discharge pipe line is open. Valve "o" in water supply line is open. Then open valve "e" next to bowl to admit necessary water. Close valve "c" and "e." After using pull lever "a."

For air expulsion

Rock air valve "f" lever outboard to charge measuring tank 10 lbs above sea pressure.

Open valve "b" and rock air valve lever inboard to blow overboard. Close valve "b." Close valve "c."

For pump expulsion
Open valve "b." Pump waste receiver empty. Close valve "b."
Close valve "c."

Piece of cake. Those directions are posted in the head of one
of the few U.S. Navy submarines that have been preserved as
maritime museums. The sign is posted on the hull behind the
toilet. That would mean if the user were in a sitting position,
he would have to crane his neck at an impossible angle to read
them or, more likely, stand up, turn around to see the directions. If the sequence was not followed correctly, the waste
could be ejected back into the head, rather than into the sea or
the vessel's sanitary tanks.

On submerged U.S. subs, human waste, as well as wastewa-
ter from bathing and the galley, was most often pumped into
the sanitary tanks for later disposal at sea or in port. Sanitation
tanks were a less elegant but no less effective solution to
relieving oneself in the deep. The German navy, increasingly
worried about detection by Allied planes and ships, designed
heads that could be flushed two hundred feet or more beneath
the waves.

The U-1206 U-boat, among the hundreds of German submarines littering the floor of the Atlantic, resting about ten
miles off Peterhead, Scotland, had what must have been the
most undistinguished record in the Kriegsmarine, having sunk
no ships other than itself on its first and only war patrol. More
embarrassing, the culprit was not some rookie swab, but the

U-boat's commander. A later model of the Type VIIC, it was equipped with a new high-pressure toilet capable of being used at great depth. Three weeks before the war in Europe ended, on April 14, 1945, the unfortunately named Kapitänleutnant Karl-Adolf Schlitt relieved himself on the high-tech head at a depth of two hundred feet. He failed to first consult with a specialist trained in its complicated operation. (The first red flag here is that a crewman was specially trained to flush the ship's toilets.) Scratching his head over how to make the darn thing work, Schlitt called in the enlisted man, who proceeded to open the wrong valve allowing—oops!—the contents of the bowl and gallons and gallons of saltwater to spew into the submarine. Schlitt might have himself been confused and given the sailor incorrect details as to what stage of the flushing process he stopped. A valve to the open sea must have been open. The surge of seawater entering the vessel was not what sent U-1206 to the bottom. Along with having an overly complex commode aboard ship, a second design flaw was situating it above the battery compartment. Saltwater reacted with the huge bank of batteries, producing deadly chlorine gas.

Schlitt ordered U-1206 to the surface to purge the hull of the poisonous fumes. This proved to be terrible timing as the sub was quickly spotted by British aircraft and attacked. Damage to the sub was such that it could not submerge, and Schlitt ordered U-1206 to be abandoned and scuttled. One sailor was killed by enemy fire; three more drowned.

"The crew reached the Scottish coast in rubber dinghies," Schlitt later wrote. "In the attempt to negotiate the steep coast in heavy seas, three crew members tragically died. Several men were taken onboard a British sloop. The dead were Hans

Berkhauer, Karl Koren and Emil Kupper." Forty-six were taken prisoner, having been plucked from the sea or captured upon making the Scottish coast.

One could believe Schlitt was the unluckiest officer in the Kriegsmarine, but was he? Despite the embarrassing circumstances of U-1206's demise, it was not the last U-boat sunk during the war. That dubious honor went to U-853, which was prowling a few miles off the coast of Rhode Island when it was pounced upon in a combined attack by destroyers and blimps on May 6, 1945. The submarine had tried hiding by lying still on the ocean floor but was detected by sonar and attacked with depth charges and hedgehogs that holed the hull. All fifty-five men aboard died twenty fathoms underwater. Two days earlier, U-853 scored the last kill of an American merchantman in the Atlantic war. Two days after U-853 sank, the war with Germany was over.

The U-boats sank more than 2,600 merchant ships totaling some thirteen million tons, as well as 175 Allied warships. Tens of thousands of sailors met their ends on those ships. But the toll on the U-boats was staggering, as well, with 784 of the 1,162 German submarines being sunk during the conflict, a loss rate of more than 64 percent. Almost forty-one thousand men were recruited to serve on U-boats, but twenty-eight thousand did not survive the war, some 68 percent, while another five thousand were taken prisoner, most when they were ordered to surrender their U-boats at the end of the war.

Karl-Adolf Schlitt died in 2009 at the age of 90. He might have felt some guilt over the next fifty-four years concerning the fate of his ship, but he was alive.

CHAPTER FIFTEEN

The Last Torpedo

"They were just laying there in the bunk, waiting to die."
—Jesse DaSilva, *Escape From the Deep*

The submarine service of the U.S. Navy fared far better than the U-boats, but the losses were very high compared to casualty figures for the rest of the Navy and the other branches of the military. Fifty-two submarines, 18 percent of the force, were lost, along with 374 officers and 3,131 enlisted men. The last U.S. submarine lost to enemy action was the USS *Bullhead* (SS-332), believed to have been depth-charged off Bali on August 6, 1945—the same day the atomic bomb was exploded over Hiroshima.

The strangest sinking, and one of the most miraculous stories of survival in the war, was the tale of the USS *Tang* (SS-306).

Commanding Officer R. H. O'Kane and a few others survived Japanese captivity to tell what happened. On October 24, 1944, while on patrol off Formosa, *Tang* launched a night surface attack against a dead-in-the-water enemy freighter, firing off one and then a second torpedo. That second fish was the last of the twenty-four torpedoes *Tang* had on board when it left Pearl Harbor. The U.S. Navy was burdened—especially early in the war—by torpedoes that often failed to hit their mark and, when they did, often failed to explode. The Mark XVIII electric torpedo was a great improvement over earlier models, but this one went rogue, either a stuck rudder or malfunctioning gyroscope being the culprit. Instead of running straight and true for the target, *Tang's* last fish instead broke the surface, then circled around and back toward the sub.

O'Kane ordered full speed and hard rudder in an attempt to evade the runaway fish. *Tang* avoided being hit amidships, but the torpedo blew off part of its stern, killing about half of the crew instantly. The force of the explosion sent O'Kane and eight other officers and men on the bridge into the sea. By the next morning, of that group only O'Kane and two others were still alive to be picked up by the Japanese, along with another officer who escaped from inside the conning tower. The fact that *Tang* was making its attack on the surface likely saved the lives of O'Kane and the others.

The sub sank stern first, settling in less than two hundred feet of water. By some miracle, about thirty men were still alive in the sub's forward compartments. Although *Tang* was dead on the seafloor, a Japanese patrol boat continued to drop depth charges to make sure of the kill. Adding to a situation that could not get much more desperate, a fire broke out in the forward battery compartment, meaning the survivors would all soon be asphyxiated by smoke and chlorine gas. The circumstances for the men trapped below were extremely dire, but where the submarine sank worked in their favor: had *Tang* been further out to sea, the ocean depth might have been such that the hull would have been crushed by the pressure, and had it settled a few fathoms deeper, the Momsen lungs designed for just this sort of emergency would have been useless. Still, the terror of attempting to escape through the chamber, first into cold, inky darkness, then up to the surface without suffering the bends, or burst lungs, was too much for about half the survivors. Clay Decker tried to persuade a crewmate to climb into the cramped escape chamber—four men could squeeze in at a time—but his friend instead crawled into his bunk.

The *USS Tang* was the deadliest submarine in the Pacific. Its last victim was most unexpected—and led to one of the most harrowing tales of escape during the war.

In Alex Kershaw's book, *Escape from the Deep*, Jesse DaSilva, one of the last to take to the chamber, later recalled seeing those who stayed behind lying in their bunks, praying or softly talking. They either waited to die from the fire and poisonous gas or took the matter into their own hands—there were enough .45-caliber pistols in the forward compartment for everyone.

Thirteen of the sailors took the only chance available, each donning a Momsen lung—a rebreathing device with a soda lime canister to absorb carbon dioxide—in their bid to escape sure death. Once inside the escape chamber, it would be flooded to equalize the pressure outside the ship, and the sailors would attempt to float slowly enough to the surface so that they would not suffer a fatal embolism. Just eight of the thirteen who chanced the escape chamber reached the surface alive, and their number dwindled to five before the Japanese plucked them from the sea, along with the four survivors from O'Kane's group. Kershaw's book, through the recollections of the few survivors and a wealth of detail on the "Silent Service," depicts a frightening scene of men choosing between sure death inside the burning *Tang* or the prospect of an agonizing death to drowning, the bends, or ruptured lungs should they attempt to make the surface.

Once all nine were aboard a destroyer, the misery continued as they were beaten by sailors who, O'Kane learned, had barely survived the sinking of their ships by *Tang*. "When we realized that our clubbings and kickings were being administered by the burned, mutilated survivors of our own handiwork, we found we could take it with less prejudice," O'Kane related after the war.

The errant torpedo put a disastrous end to the most successful combat patrol of the Pacific War, as *Tang* sent thirteen ships totaling more than one hundred thousand tons to the bottom before she torpedoed herself. In her five patrols, *Tang* was credited with sinking thirty-one Japanese ships weighing in at more than 227,000 tons. O'Kane and the other eight crewmen survived being prisoners of war to return home, where the *Tang's* skipper was awarded the Medal of Honor. *Tang* and seventy-eight crewmen remain on eternal patrol.

CHAPTER SIXTEEN
Corporal Wojtek

"I'm smarter than the average bear."

—Yogi Bear

"If you don't know where you are going, you might wind up someplace else."

—Yogi Berra

Corporal Wojtek had a lot in common with his fellow soldiers: a taste for cold beer, smoking, raiding the mess tent for snacks, and a little horseplay during downtime in camp. But this dogface was different from the other members of his unit. He sometimes ate lit cigarettes and, tipping the scales at about five hundred pounds, he didn't lose a wrestling match unless it was his idea.

Sixteen days after the September 1, 1939, Nazi invasion of Poland, the Soviet Union—with a wink and a nod from Hitler—invaded Eastern Poland. German Foreign Minister Joachim von Ribbentrop and his Soviet counterpart Vyacheslav Molotov inked a nonaggression pact between the two dictatorships in August, sealing Poland's fate. The Red Army had little trouble rolling up what was left of the Polish Army, and a few hundred thousand Polish soldiers were taken as prisoners of war, though Wojtek (pronounced Voy-Teck) was not among them.

Less than two years later, on June 22, 1941, Hitler unceremoniously pulled out of the Molotov-Ribbentrop Pact by invading his erstwhile ally to the east. Poles in Soviet custody (many in gulag labor camps) were allowed to form military units to combat the Germans—the Polish I Corps and II Corps, the latter being transferred in 1943 to serve with British forces in the Middle East. The tens of thousands of Poles who volunteered to fight with the Western Allies made the long journey—much of it on foot—to Palestine through Iran, which is where Wojtek's tale begins.

While en route to Tehran from a Soviet gulag, a group of Poles came upon a shepherd boy in the mountains carrying a sack with something squirming inside—an orphaned Syrian brown bear cub with which the boy wanted to barter. The Poles offered up rations, candy bars, and a pocketknife to acquire the baby bear. The soldiers were traveling with civilian refugees, and one of them, Irena Bokiewicz, adopted the beast as a pet until he grew to be too much of a responsibility. The soldiers took over the cub's care and used improvised nipples on empty vodka bottles filled with condensed milk solutions to wean the baby bear. Wojtek, the bear, slept on a soldier's chest at night. To see photographs of the cub shortly after the trade, one can see why the soldiers wanted him as a mascot— he really was adorable!

The fuzzy little cubby accompanied the men as their unit, the 22nd Artillery Support Company, moved first to the Middle East, then on to the Italian campaign. But little bear cubs become big adult bears, and Wojtek did just that, growing into a quarter-ton beast, while still maintaining his good nature.

"He adored fights with other soldiers and even fought with four opponents at the same time," said Archibald Brown, a British courier who witnessed a bout between Wojtek and a few of his comrades. "He hid his claws and skated with them on the floor, braked them, and pretended that he was going to bite. But he never offended anyone."

"He would accept lit cigarettes, take a puff and swallow them," Dymitr Szawlugo, one of the soldiers assigned to keep an eye on Wojtek, recalled after the war. "He loved to drink from a beer bottle, and when it was empty, he would look through the opening to see where the rest of the beer was."

The latter sounds like behavior he emulated from other beer lovers. As with a dog learning to fetch or sit in exchange for a treat, Wojtek initially earned his beer ration by learning to salute.

Dogs, cats, goats, and monkeys were among the animals adopted as mascots by military units of all service branches and countries, having the benefit of being domesticated, or at least easy to care for or train. But a mascot the size of Wojtek presented special challenges, one of which was moving a huge wild animal from one theater to another. To get the behemoth onto a British transport from Egypt to Italy, his comrades came up with the idea of giving him the rank of private, along with assigning him a serial number and issuing a paybook in his name. The ruse likely did not fool the Brit sailors, but they went along with the gag. He was later "promoted" to corporal.

During the Italian campaign, II Corps took part in the 1944 battle of attrition between the Allies and the Germans holding the monastery of Monte Cassino. After weeks of aerial bombardments, endless artillery barrages, and unsuccessful infantry assaults, it was the Poles who finally wrested from the Germans the pile of rubble that was once Monte Cassino. Wojtek became famous during the siege for actions that sound too good to be true.

Left unattended, but chained to a truck, Wojtek once again emulated his fellow soldiers, this time during battle. In what might be an apocryphal story, Wojtek saw his fellow soldiers moving crates of ammunition from the truck, somehow slipped his chain, and began to do the same. Handling the weight would not have been a problem—bears are rather strong after all—but staggering around on his hind legs while carting about boxes of ammo or individual shells seems a stretch.

What gives this tale some credence is the unit patch for the 22nd Artillery Support Company—the outline of a bear carrying an artillery shell. True or not, the story screams "Disney movie!"

With the end of the war, many of the Poles who served II Corps found themselves in Great Britain, with the fate of their homeland in the hands of the same Soviets who took them as prisoners of war in 1939. Wojtek was with them, living at an aerodrome in Berwickshire, Scotland. The corps was demobilized in 1947, and Wojtek's comrades felt it better to leave their beloved mascot in Scotland rather than take him back to their home behind the Iron Curtain. No longer a member of the Polish Army, the veteran retired and settled down to life in the Edinburgh Zoo. Former comrades would occasionally visit, even going into his enclosure to relive their glory days with an impromptu wrestling match. Wojtek still loved a cold bottle of suds and the occasional smoke, and he became a popular attraction at the zoo.

"My dad used to take me to see him. He told me to speak Polish to him and his head would turn," Izabella Brodzinka (who later became chairwoman of the Scottish Polish Cultural Association) recalled in a 2007 article in *The Scotsman*. "He was a lovely big bear, very sad looking, but when you spoke Polish to him he turned and made a sound. He missed the Polish soldiers."

He also missed tobacco. In the same article, Aileen Orr, who coauthored a book about the bear, recalled Wojtek holding out "a paw the size of a soup plate" when her grandfather offered him a lit cigarette at the zoo. Wojtek lived out his life at Edinburgh Zoo, dying in 1963 at the relatively young age of twenty-one—perhaps a victim of the vices he acquired in the Polish Army, but more likely for lack of camaraderie.

Wojtek was gone but not long forgotten. In 2014 a statue of the soldier bear was unveiled in a park in Krakow, Poland, marking the 70th anniversary of the Battle of Monte Cassino.

A year later, he was immortalized in bronze in Edinburgh's West Princess Street Gardens.

One can follow the life of Wojtek on the Internet, both in articles and photos that document his ursine adventures from cuddly cub to beer-guzzling combat veteran. There's even some old film of his wrestling harmlessly with a fellow soldier at some desert encampment.

****

To judge by the newsreels, every German soldier in World War II rode into battle on a panzer, or at the very least, in a Kübelwagen, the Wehrmacht version of the Volkswagen Beetle. The reality was much different for the men who slogged along in nonmechanized infantry divisions. For those *soldaten,* transportation was a train ride to the depot nearest the front, followed by a long march toward the sound of guns. German artillery was more often than not hauled by horses, not trucks.

Not long after the first animals were domesticated, man found some adaptable to warfare. Since men learned to ride horses and then to hitch them to chariots, equines have fought, suffered, and died. They have been butchered in the millions by spear and sword, musket and cannon, heat and cold, and starvation, disease, and exhaustion. The difference between man and animal is that a horse has no understanding of why its guts have been spilled, or its leg blown off. It only experiences pain, fear, and death, never knowing what god, king, country, or -ism it gave its life for.

Some eight million horses were used by the Allies and Central Powers during World War I, and throughout the Second

World War the armies of Germany, the Soviet Union, and Japan depended heavily on animal transport. The equine complement for an eighteen thousand–man German infantry division was more than four thousand animals, all of which required feed, tack, and veterinary care. The United States and Great Britain for the most part rode into battle in trucks and jeeps.

For America's horses, World War II was a blessing. The Remount Branch estimated in 1939 the U.S. military would need two hundred thousand horses to meet its needs once the country entered the war. The reality was that the American military effectively retired the horse, with the remaining cavalry units in the regular Army and National Guard converting to motorized transport. The armed forces purchased 23,546 horses in 1941, a number that fell to 2,859 the following year. Having plenty of horses without jobs, the military branches purchased just four in 1943 and none in either of the following two years. From 1942 on, the military was saddled with the problem of reducing, often by sale, its four-hooved inventory. Anna L. Waller wrote the following in a 1958 Office of the Quartermaster General article:

"Throughout the war period the problem of the Remount Branch, insofar as horses were concerned, was chiefly a matter of liquidation rather than of procurement. This situation began to develop after Pearl Harbor when animal-using organizations were ordered de-horsed because the units were needed overseas immediately and no shipping space was available for movement of their animals," according to a 1958 Office of the Quartermaster General article written by Mrs. Anna L. Waller. "The large-scale dismounting of these units began in the spring of 1942 when seven fed-eralized National Guard horse-mechanized regiments and the 6th Cavalry Regiment were directed to turn in their animals. Similar orders were issued to various other units in the following months. The 1st Cavalry Division was de-horsed during April and May 1943, and finally the 2nd Cavalry Division and the 56th Brigade of the Texas National Guard in March 1944."

However, it was true that a mule could go just about any place a man could walk, and places no tank, truck, or jeep could venture. Thus the numbers for mule purchases went in a differ-ent direction. The branches bought 4,279 mules in 1941, but the number fell to 1,699 in 1942. Real war experience showed that, in the near-impenetrable jungles of Southeast Asia, the China-Burma-India theater, the Pacific islands, or in the mountainous terrain of Italy, the mule was invaluable for hauling ammuni-tion, weapons, and supplies of all kinds. Mule purchases rose to 10,217 in 1943. The number fell by half to 5,129 in 1944, but the military procured 9,199 in 1945. Lucky for those 30,000 mules, most stayed stateside. Seventy-eight hundred pack ani-mals went to U.S. forces overseas, and the British acquired 3,500 under Lend Lease. Many more were procured overseas, partic-ularly in Italy, which also supplied the U.S. Army with thou-sands of mule skinners—men who already knew how to handle donkeys and mules and who knew the terrain. The reasons for overseas procurement were logical enough as Waller explained:

There were several reasons why more pack mules were procured abroad than were sent to the theaters from the United States. One of these, of course, was that it was extremely difficult to obtain shipping space for the animals and their forage. Another was that requirements for animals in the theaters, particularly in the early stages of the war, were not anticipated sufficiently in advance to enable shipments to be made. In this connection there appears to have existed even in the minds of many early planners in the War Department an implicit faith in the ability of mechanized forces to move over all types of terrain, and apparently this faith persisted until the troops in the field actually began to encounter rugged mountains in which motor vehicles simply could not operate. In any case, it is obvious that no adequate advance plans were made for the use of pack mules overseas nor for the training of personnel to handle and care for the animals.

Wherever the soldier could go but a Jeep could not, the U.S. Army mule proved its worth, from the mountains of Italy to the jungles of Burma and New Guinea.

One four-legged veteran of World War II was still fighting six years later—but for the other side—in the Korean War. The animal was among the mules liberated as American forces pushed the Chinese Communists and North Koreans north in 1951, according to the American Mule Museum:

> One of the captured mules was of particular interest, as it was found to have a U.S. army Brand (a Preston Brand) number 08K0. When that brand was located in the Army records, it was found that he had been originally dispatched to the China-Burma-India theater during WWII. Following that war, the mule was transferred to the Chinese Army. He must have been later captured by the Communist Chinese, and then moved to the fight in Korea. After more than six years, that mule ended up back in the hands of the U.S. Army—then returned to work on a pack train.

No rest for the weary.

The U.S. Army deactivated its last two operational mule units at Fort Carson, Colorado, on February 15, 1957. However, special-forces units would later use these tough, stubborn, and versatile beasts of burden in the rugged mountains of Afghanistan in operations against the Taliban and al Qaeda.

Stateside, this icon of the Army is mostly relegated to mascot duty for the U.S. Military Academy's football games, braying noisily on the sidelines when an Army touchdown triggers a report from a small cannon located off the end zone.

CHAPTER SEVENTEEN
Desperate Times, Dumb Ideas

"This is the patent age of new inventions for killing bodies, and for saving souls."

—Lord Byron

The laboratory of war has produced astounding advances in science—most of them horrible. The atomic bomb and napalm in World War II are just two examples on that side of the ledger. On the other hand, the war brought speedy advances in radar, sonar, aeronautics, and medicine, which have saved lives and improved safety, or at least made life more convenient. The ubiquitous microwave oven came about as a result of an accidental discovery during radar research.

However, most experiments reach dead ends. As Thomas Edison may or may not have said, "Results! Why, man, I have gotten a lot of results! I know several thousand things that won't work."

In the contest for world domination, all the major combatants furiously worked to develop weapons that would give them an edge on land, sea, and air. The United States, with Herculean efforts, came up with the one absolute war-winning weapon, the atomic bomb. Some weapon systems gave the Western Allies, Soviets, Germans, and Japanese an upper hand in some aspect of warfare. These nations also expended—really wasted—great amounts of treasure on weapons that were ill-conceived, ineffective, poorly made, and often more dangerous to the users than their enemies.

The worst days for the British, Russians, and Americans were from 1939 to mid-1943. The Germans and Japanese were not going to win after el Alamein, Stalingrad, and Midway. Instead of calling for peace talks, the Nazis and Japanese doubled down, believing there was some way they could prevail, or at least continue to exist. There wasn't, at least not in a way that could preserve their political and cultural polity.

The law of unintended consequences might have doomed the Nazi regime as much as anything: many of their finest scientists were Jewish and fled the regime—to the benefit of the United States, which committed wholeheartedly to the atomic bomb.

But there was more. The weight of arms and population were against the Germans and the Japanese. For crying out loud, Hitler decided to declare war on the United States four days after Pearl Harbor, instead of waiting and hoping America would only commit to a Pacific war.

How were 80 million Germans (including Austria and the Sudetenland) and 44 million unmotivated Italians going to defeat 47 million British (not counting Canada, Australia, India, and a few dozen more Commonwealth members and colonies), 170 million Russians, and 132 million Americans? How were 73 million Japanese supposed to subjugate 500 million Chinese and overcome the industrial might of the United States?

Short of the British suing for peace during the Battle of Britain, the Russians calling it quits in the first months of Operation Barbarossa, and the United States calling it even-steven with the Japanese after sinking four carriers at Midway, the Axis was not going to win the war. Eventually, the weight of populations and arms production would have prevailed, regardless of what wonder weapons the Germans came up with.

Just on armored production, the USSR, United States, and United Kingdom cranked out north of 176,000 tanks to the Germans' 50,000 tanks and tracked vehicles with guns mounted in fixed casemates (the German number including about 12,000 of these assault guns), as well as about 6,500 PzKpfw I and II models, which were outdated before the war started. Germany could not have won the war, but had it chosen to concentrate on upgrading proven technology, it could have prolonged the killing, perhaps by months with the loss of a few hundred thousand more lives—soldiers and civilians—on all sides. The Japanese clock was going to run out with the dropping of atomic bombs on Hiroshima and Nagasaki, regardless of what wonder weapons they might have developed.

The more desperate a nation's straits, the more effort and resources it wastes on chasing a miracle weapon. Here are some examples from all sides.

Panzerkampfwagen I, II, and III

The Panzerkampfwagen I, II, and III comprised the bulk of armored vehicles in the Wehrmacht at the war's outbreak. The Germans built about three thousand of the PzKpfw I, which was armed only with machine guns and was too thin-skinned for combat. More than 3,500 of the PzKpfw IIs, armed with a twenty-millimeter cannon and a machine gun, were produced and proved of little use in the field, although many were later converted into self-propelled guns with larger caliber cannon mounted in a fixed casemate. The PzKpfw III started the war with a short-barreled thirty-seven-millimeter gun, later upped to a longer-barreled fifty-millimeter cannon, still just a "door knocker" against T-34s. The Panzer IIs and IIIs made up the majority of armored vehicles deployed with combat units in 1939, with the PzKpfw IV just starting to roll off the assembly lines. These four-series tanks were the panzers that swept across Western Europe in 1940 and deep into Russia in 1941-42, but it was more a triumph of tactics and training than technology. Germany continued to produce IIIs until 1943, instead of focusing production on IVs. In particular with the invasion of the Soviet Union, the German land forces had far fewer machines than the Red Army, and the Russian vehicles were superior in fundamental respects.

Before the war the Soviets purchased experimental tanks designed by American J. Walter Christie that offered innovations the Russians took to heart in producing their own designs: the helicoil suspension and sloped armor. The former gave his designs superior performance on roads and cross-country, whereas the latter increased shot deflection and resistance to penetration. The U.S. Army thought his designs too expensive, so Christie sold them overseas. The Russians improved on his ideas, culminating in the T-34, which was being deployed in small numbers just as the Germans were gearing up to invade. But the majority of Soviet tanks were of earlier designs—they had BT-26s by the thousands—and the Germans bagged thousands of Red Army tanks and hundreds of thousands of prisoners through their superior leadership and training. Panzer IIs and IIIs were undergunned and lacked the performance of Soviet tanks, but a well-crewed Panzer IV had a decent chance on the battlefield against a T-34.

The Germans up-gunned and up-armored the Panzer IV throughout the war, while waiting until 1943 to finally drop production of the Panzer III. The Germans then developed and produced the two designs they felt could stem the red tide—the Panther and Tiger. It might have been more efficient to continue the Panzer IV upgrades, concentrate on Panther production and forget the Tiger altogether. Tiger I and Tiger II (the latter known as "King" or "Royal" Tigers) production amounted to fewer than 1,900, compared to nearly 9,000 Panzer IVs and about 6,000 Panthers. The knock on the Tiger is not that it was ineffective—in a defensive role it was almost unbeatable. But it was plagued by suspension, transmission, and engine problems that limited its offensive capabilities as the designers tried to hang more armor onto the chassis—nearly seventy tons in the end. Tigers also absorbed huge amounts of valuable commodities, production capacity, and skilled labor that could have been devoted to building more, albeit smaller, tanks.

L3 and M13

The Italian L3 was "a machine unworthy of the word 'tank,'" according to one writer, and he was on the mark. Fiat built

these underpowered, underarmored, and pitifully undergunned machines based on an earlier, and outmoded, British
Vickers design. It was the mainstay of Italian armored units in
North Africa but could and did fall prey to aggressive infantry
tactics by Ethiopians and, later, the British. One British officer, Major James Hill, was credited with capturing two Italian
tanks by charging them and firing his pistol into their view-
ports. He was wounded attempting to capture a third. Because
the Italians padded the L3s with insufficient armor, Hill probably bagged a pair of two-man tankettes. The L3 was armed
with a pair of machine guns with a limited traverse, and the
three-ton vehicle puttered along at a speedy 25 mph—on a
good road—if the forty-three-horsepower engine was working
that day. The armor was just thirteen millimeters at its thick-
est, a skin unlikely to stop a round from a heavy machine gun.

The Italians had a medium tank, the M13, which had an
actual turret to house its forty-seven-millimeter cannon. It was
designed to accompany infantry assaults so had an incredibly
slow 9-mph cross-country speed, making it a sitting duck for
British gunners and tank crews.

Me 163 and Me 262

The Messerschmitt Me 163 Komet was the only rocket-powered
fighter aircraft of the war; it successfully killed a number of
Luftwaffe pilots while knocking down a few Allied bombers.
The Komet could outperform any Allied fighter by about two
hundred miles per hour—for a short time. The Me 163 was so
fast—more than six hundred miles per hour—that pilots had
difficulty aiming the aircraft's slow-firing thirty-millimeter
cannon on a target and getting off a few rounds before zoom-
ing past a lumbering B-17 or Lancaster bomber. The difference

in speed between Komet and target could be as much as 350 mph. The Germans produced 370 Me 163s, which downed perhaps nine Allied bombers. About as many of the rocket fighters were lost to Allied fighters and one to a sharpshooting (or lucky) B-17 tailgunner. Fourteen Me 163's were lost in accidents or to other causes. Operationally, the plane could not be fueled until just before a mission, as its C-Stoff fuel and T-Stoff oxidizer were extremely volatile and required special handling. On takeoff, the pilot dropped the Komet's two-wheeled dolly and, on landing, deployed a retractable skid with a shock absorber. While it could reach the altitude of bomber formations in a matter of minutes, a Komet could only use its motor for power or glide for a short time before having to make a dead-stick landing to an airfield or pasture smooth enough. As it came home without power and at a very high speed, getting the landing right on the first approach was a life-and-death matter.

The Me 163 rocket fighter likely killed more Germans than Allies.

Famed Nazi test pilot Hanna Reitsch discovered how dangerous the Komet was to fly. On a glide test, a crewman in the
tow plane alerted her that the two-wheel dolly had failed to
disengage. The dolly created a great deal of turbulence and,
when she cut the towline, she was barely able to maintain control. The unpowered aircraft stalled about a hundred feet above
ground and the impact fractured her skull in several places and
dislocated her jaw. One pilot on a powered test flight fractured
enough vertebrae on landing to require a year's recuperation
in a hospital.

Remaining oxidizer in the pressurized tanks right behind
the cockpit could and did ignite on a rough landing. Fueling
the swept-winged Komet was almost as deadly as flying it: The
alcohol and hydrazine hydrate fuel (C-Stoff) and hydrogen
peroxide oxidizer (T-Stoff) were dangerously volatile alone or
in combination. Each had to be transported in separate trucks
with handlers wearing protective clothing, and each chemical was just itching for an excuse to explode. The hydrogen
peroxide was not the highly diluted type people use to clean
out their ears or wash a cut—the concentration was 97 to 99
percent.

"T-Stoff and C-Stoff were both colorless fluids, and on
one occasion an unfortunate mechanic poured a few pints of
the latter into a bucket containing a minute quantity of the
former," William Green wrote in *Rocket Fighter*. The resulting
explosion left the man's remains "spread thinly over the entire
test shed."

On December 30, 1943, Oberleutnant Josef Pohs rendered his New Year's plans moot with a test flight of the Komet
163A. He got his death trap airborne but released the dolly at

too low an altitude. The dolly bounced back up and struck the Komet, which pitched up a few hundred feet before banking back toward the field for a very hard landing. According to Green, Pohs had apparently been knocked unconscious "and had then literally been dissolved alive by the T-Stoff that seeped into the cockpit" from a broken fuel line.

Feldwebel Alios Wörndl piloted a Komet during testing and Leutnant Mano Ziegler witnessed the outcome of his comrade's final flight. Wörndl's landing approach was too high and too fast:

> We watched with horror as it floated away across the airfield as if some invisible hand was holding the aircraft away from the safety of the runway. Anxiously we watched the Komet touch down far outside the airfield perimeter, rebound back up into the air, drop back again like a brick, and then skid into some rough ground and turn over on its back. A split-second later a blinding white flame shot up, followed by a mushroom of smoke.

The fuel and oxidizer were also more difficult to produce than the other synthetic fuels the Germans increasingly relied upon as their empire shrank, leaving many Komets sitting useless on tarmacs, in fields, or in hangars. The aircraft needed a specially designed tractor to haul it to and from its launch site, making it that much more of an impractical weapon. Thank goodness the Germans spent so much time, research, and resources chasing tactical advantages rather than strategic ones—like an atomic bomb.

The twin-engine, swept-winged Me 262 Schwalbe (Swallow) proved less fatal to its pilots, and its performance exceeded 500 mph, while having much greater endurance than the Komet. Hitler supposedly ordered that it be adapted as a bomber, rather like putting a thoroughbred in front of a plow. After a few months, the dictator's diktat was overruled, and the Swallow proved its effectiveness against B-17s late in the war—too late to make any real difference. It is unlikely that swarms of Swallows could have done much to blunt the bomber offensive, as fighter escorts learned to ambush the jets, either as they were taking off or on landing. As with many later war innovations, the Me 262 was developed too little, too late, while also plagued by frequent engine failures and other teething troubles from being rushed into production.

The Germans had more success with the V-1 cruise missile and the V-2 ballistic rocket, but even these proved only of use as terror weapons, being too few and absorbing too much in materials and skilled labor to tip the strategic balance. Had that effort been diverted to production of the Me 262, it would have made the Allied bombing campaign even more prohibitively expensive in lives and machinery.

Kamikaze

A. J. Barker's book *Suicide Weapon* has on its cover a photo of a kamikaze pilot tying a ceremonial *hachimaki* cloth around his head prior to taking off for his (presumably) last mission. The weapon of the book's title was in fact the Japanese soldier, sailor, or airman all too willing to embody the Bushido spirit and sacrifice himself for the honor of the Chrysanthemum Throne of Emperor Hirohito. "Death before dishonor" was no idle boast on the part of Japanese servicemen, and their leaders did their level best to find creative ways for their warriors to off themselves, often giving poetic names to these devices and tactics of self-destruction.

Kamikaze, as just about everyone knows, means "divine wind"; it dates back in Japanese history to typhoons that swept away Mongol invasion fleets in 1274 and 1281. In October 1944, Vice Admiral Takijiro Onishi established the Kamikaze Special-Attack Corps in the Philippines in hope of using his meager air resources to buy as many American lives as cheaply as possible. "Kamikaze" was applied primarily to the land-based pilots who dove their warplanes into U.S. warships and transports. The Special Attack Corps and its successors sank or damaged scores of ships and killed and wounded thousands of sailors during the final year of the war, still far short of what was needed to slow the American juggernaut.

Ohka

The Japanese had their own rocket plane, the Ohka, or "cherry blossom," a name that might have been meant to describe the fiery bloom it was supposed to make upon slamming into an American ship. Not a fighter like the Komet, the Ohka was a rocket-powered manned bomb launched from the belly of a twin-engine Mitsubishi G4M "Betty" bomber. The Ohka's four solid-fuel rocket motors would speed its pilot and a 2,600-pound warhead into enemy vessels—or that was the idea. An Ohka hit and damaged the battleship *West Virginia* in March 1945, and later attacks heavily damaged a few transports. The Achilles' heel of the Ohka was that it had to be air-launched within about twenty-five miles of a target. Combat air patrols ranged much further out from carrier task forces to search for and intercept threats to the flat tops. An external bomb load of more than two tons just meant the Betty, already no match for a fighter, lost even more speed and maneuverability. The end result was often the loss of the Betty and its crew, along with the Ohka and its pilot. Americans had a more apt name for the Ohka, calling it the *Baka*, Japanese for "fool." On the first Ohka mission, all eighteen Bettys and their Ohka bomb loads were lost to Grumman Hellcats. Many of the Betty pilots jettisoned their payloads in fruitless efforts to escape being shot down, thus sending the Ohka pilots to an even more pointless death, too far away to reach a target. Of the 750 or so Ohkas built by the end of the war, only a fraction were sent into combat, and the results were not worth the industrial effort and loss of life. Fifty of the rocket planes bound for the Philippines were lost on November 29, 1944, when the USS *Archerfish* sank the supercarrier *Shinano* on its maiden voyage.

Kaiten

The Imperial Navy had its own martyr-making invention, the Kaiten, meaning "heaven shaker," a Type 93 torpedo modified to be launched from the deck of a submerged I-class submarine. The long-range, speedy Type 93 proved itself deadly against U.S. warships early in the war, especially when launched by surface ships during night attacks. By adding a pilot's compartment, diving planes, rudimentary controls, gauges, and a periscope, the Kaiten torpedo proved an effective weapon for killing its pilots and the crews of its submarine mother ships. It sank a U.S. tanker and a large landing craft while damaging a few other vessels, but many more Japanese died during operations. Kaiten's first victim was one of its designers, a naval officer named Hiroshi Kuroki, who got his torpedo stuck in an underwater mud bank during testing. Six more died in training.

Up to six Kaiten could be lashed to the deck of an I-class submarine, which would bring them into the proximity of a target or targets. The mother ship would maneuver into position and the Kaiten pilots, sealed within their coffins, would receive instructions via a telephone link from the sub's conning tower to each human torpedo. The Kaitens would be released from the deck at short intervals and take off on individual headings. Following instructions they received before the telephone link was broken, the pilots would follow their headings for a designated time at a designated speed. Five hundred yards from the target—if the pilot had received accurate directions—he would put up the Kaiten's periscope and set a final course for impact.

On November 20, 1944, the I-47 and I-36 loosed five of the eight Kaiten they carried on the U.S. fleet harbored at Ulithi. I-47 was able to release all its human torpedoes, but the release mechanisms for two of the craft on I-36 failed to work, and the pilot of a third reported his torpedo was leaking badly. The submarines returned to Japan, their crews believing the Kaitens had taken out several ships based on the explosions they heard. However, only one Kaiten found a target, destroying a tanker, the USS *Mississinewa*.

Kaitens sank and damaged a few small warships and transports before the war ended, but many pilots drowned when their torpedoes ran out of propellant and sank to the bottom, or were sunk by antisubmarine patrols. Several of the mother submarines, slowed by the cargo strapped to their decks, became easy prey for destroyers and went down with all hands. Eventually, there were not enough submarines left to take the Kaitens into harm's way. Plans to launch the torpedoes from shore bases to attack an expected U.S. invasion fleet were frustrated by the war's end, thus saving many Imperial sailors from an honorable death.

Yamato

The battleship Yamato became Japan's most massive suicide weapon in another act of pointless sacrifice. At 64,000 tons and armed with nine 18.1-inch guns, *Yamato* and its sister ship *Musashi* were expected to play pivotal roles in the "decisive battle" the Imperial Navy always sought, but never achieved, against the U.S. Navy. *Musashi* was overwhelmed by twenty aerial torpedo strikes and another seventeen hits from dive bombers before it sank in the Sibuyan Sea in October 1944. Eleven months later, *Yamato* was loaded with enough scarce diesel oil for a one-way voyage to Okinawa where it was to pound the American fleet and transports landing troops and supplies on the island.

On April 6, 1944, *Yamato* and nine other ships, designated as the Second Fleet, set sail from Japan's Inland Sea. Two days later, three hundred American carrier planes attacked the Second Fleet, sinking *Yamato* and five of its escorts in a hailstorm of bombs and torpedoes. In all, 2,500 Japanese sailors gave their lives for nothing.

****

When the fight for a Pacific island was a lost cause, Japanese officers made sure their losses were maximized. Soldiers and marines huddled in bunkers and caves would be rallied to rush out for one last, hopeless and pointless banzai charge from which few or none would survive. Ironically, banzai is a sort of Japanese shorthand for "may you live ten thousand years."

In banzai charges, kamikaze attacks, Kaiten sorties, and other fruitless assaults, Japanese soldiers, airmen, and sailors lived up to the words of their "Warrior's Song":

> In serving on the seas, be a corpse saturated with water,
> In serving on land, be a corpse covered with weeds,
> But we have nothing to regret so long as we die fighting for our Emperor.

Emperor Hirohito lived to the age of 87, always having a palace to call home. He may have felt guilty from time to time in the more than four decades he lived past the war's end, but millions died for him while he sacrificed nothing.

The United States, Britain, and Russia produced outstanding designs in huge numbers. The United States, in particular, fielded the war's finest prop-driven fighters, particularly the P-51 Mustang. The RAF had to be persuaded to accept the outstanding Spitfire and Mosquito, while the Lancaster heavy bomber was the result of adding longer wings and an additional two Merlin engines to a failed twin-engine design. The

Soviets fielded the best all-around tank in the T-34, and the best airborne tank destroyer in the Shturmovik.

Boulton Paul Defiant

The Allies had their share of bad designs that made their way to the battlefields. The Boulton Paul Defiant defied both the laws of aerodynamics and common sense. The British figured a fighter would be more effective if its guns could be aimed in more directions than just straight ahead. They were confident the Defiant was the answer, with its four .30-caliber machine guns mounted in a powered, manned turret just behind the cockpit. The thinking of the designers was wrong on two major counts: Adding another man and the turret machinery just made the plane that much heavier, and the drag created by the turret made it harder to push the whole contraption through the air. It also lacked maneuverability. A pilot could nudge the Defiant just above 300 mph, a deadly deficit of speed when it encountered Me 109s over France in 1940. The Defiant had some success early on until Messerschmitt pilots figured out it was defenseless against attacks from the front (it had no fixed, wing-mounted machine guns) or below. Then it was easy meat for the Germans. Defiant pilots found themselves trying to defend themselves rather than take on the enemy. The best tactic when confronted by 109s was to bank into a descending circle and ride out an attack as the turret gunner tried to keep the enemy in his sights. Similar to the German's twin-engine Me 110 fighter, the Defiant could take on lumbering enemy bombers until their fighter escorts arrived to save the day. Hawker Hurricanes and Supermarine Spitfires often flew to the rescue of outmatched Defiants. The British produced 1,054

Defiants before cutting their losses—of both planes and crews. The Defiant did respectable service after that as a night fighter taking on German bombers—most effectively from below and behind—before being withdrawn from service in 1942.

M4 Sherman

At times it can be difficult to tell whether a weapon system was poorly conceived, poorly utilized, or both. The M4 Sherman had a mixed reputation: Defenders cite its mechanical reliability, 25-mph speed, good cross-country performance, and crew-friendly interior layout; critics would point to its inadequate armor protection, reputation for catching fire, and a seventy-five-millimeter gun that lacked the muzzle velocity to trade punches with Panthers and Tigers. Both sides have their points. The Sherman matched up well with the more numerous Panzer IVs, and its propensity to catch fire (common to just about any tank when hit) was greatly reduced by water-jacketing ammunition storage in later models. The seventy-five-millimeter gun was later changed out for a high-velocity seventy-six-millimeter canon beginning in 1944. Still, Shermans were destroyed in large numbers, particularly when advancing against a well dug-in Tiger.

The M4's greatest virtue was that more than fifty thousand were produced in the United States and Canada. Its other great virtue was the versatility of the tank and its chassis. The British adapted the Sherman in a number of ways, such as modifying the turret to accommodate its seventeen-pound, antitank gun. The Sherman could be mounted with mine flails, dozer blades, and *bocage* shredding teeth. Despite its thirty-five tons, the M4 was also modified into duplex drive (DD) amphibious tanks.

A collapsible canvas skirt raised on a metal frame allowed DD Shermans to float, although that ability should not be confused with seaworthiness. Skirt up and propellers engaged, the DDs could churn through light swells or cross a river at just 4 mph. Proof that the DDs were poorly designed and poorly deployed can be found littering the seabed off Normandy.

On D-Day the 741st Armored Battalion launched twenty-nine DD Shermans from LCTs (landing craft tanks) four kilometers off Omaha Beach in support of the infantry already under punishing German artillery and machine-gun fire. Twenty-seven of the tanks sank, a sight that caused the 743rd Armored Battalion to cancel its sea launch and instead land its tanks directly onto the beach.

The first mistake was developing a tank that would perform so poorly in an amphibious role: slow, hard to maneuver, and reliant on a sheet of canvas to keep it from foundering. The second was launching them so far out at sea, making the journey to shore nearly an hour long if all went well. The third thing that did not go well was the weather, which whipped up six-foot seas. The DDs were designed to waddle their way through one-foot swells.

Fortunately, most of the crews were reported to have been saved. The losses at Sword, Juno, and Utah beaches were less disastrous due to calmer seas and lighter German resistance. At Utah, four were lost when their LCT was sunk by artillery. Of the rest, launched much closer to shore than at Omaha, twenty-seven of twenty-eight made it to the beach.

The seamanship of the tank crews at Omaha was also lacking, perhaps due to inadequate training. Most of the tanks—the ones that sank—headed straight for the landing area, exposing the sides of the DDs to a beam sea. The force of the waves damaged the flotation skirts and the metal frames causing them to quickly become swamped and lose what little buoyancy they had. The two tanks that made it to shore had commanders with enough boating experience to keep their sterns to the waves.

"Numerous reports criticizing the performance of the DD-Tanks were prepared by the training battalions in England, but never reached the upper echelons of command," according to a 2012 BBC article.

Douglas TDB-1 Devastator

Even an inferior weapon could prove itself pivotal in battle when in the hands of brave and determined men. The Douglas TDB-1 Devastator helped change the tide of the Pacific war, albeit at great sacrifice to its crews.

On the morning of June 4, 1942, fifteen Devastators lumbered off the deck of the carrier *Hornet* in search of the Japanese fleet attacking the American base at Midway Island. Fourteen more Devastators took off from *Enterprise*.

The Devastator had a top speed of about 200 mph but was much slower with a torpedo slung under its belly. The torpedo bomber's lackluster performance made it easy prey for the Imperial Japanese Navy's Zero fighters.

When the Devastator squadrons spotted the four Japanese carriers, they descended to a few dozen feet above sea level to begin their attacks. This attracted both the Zeros already in the air and the antiaircraft guns of every ship.

All fifteen of the Devastators from *Hornet* were shot down. Only one of the thirty men in those planes, Ensign George H. Gay, survived the fight, watching the ensuing events unfold while clinging to his flotation device.

The bloodletting for the squadron from *Enterprise* was almost as bad: ten of the planes were shot down. For this loss of men and machines not one Devastator managed to launch a torpedo that found a target. Yet their sacrifice was not by any means in vain.

The attack absorbed the attention of the Japanese, including bringing all the Zeros down to sea level to slaughter the Devastators. Unnoticed by the Japanese until it was too late was the approach from high altitude of Douglas SBD Dauntless dive bombers.

On the decks of the enemy carriers, crews were fueling and arming aircraft for a strike on the American task force. With the Zeros at low level chasing off what was left of the Devastators, the carriers were sitting ducks. In a handful of minutes *Akagi*, *Kaga*, and *Soryu* were flaming wrecks.

An attack the same afternoon would doom the fourth Japanese carrier, *Hiryu*. Six months earlier, all four of the carriers had taken part in the attack on Pearl Harbor. The loss of these ships, as well as their experienced air crews, was a setback from which the Imperial Japanese Navy would never recover.

Chapter Eighteen
A Final Accounting

"But many that are first shall be last; and the last shall be first."

—Matthew 19:30

Just before 0800 hours, a Japanese Imperial Navy strike force of forty-three Zeros, forty Nakajima B5N2 "Kate" torpedo bombers, forty-nine more Kates armed with armor-piercing bombs for high-level attack, and fifty-one Aichi D3A1 "Val" dive bombers descended on Pearl Harbor, the Kate torpedo bombers lining up for a low-level attack on "Battleship Row." Outboard of the USS *Maryland*, the USS *Oklahoma* absorbed several torpedo hits from torpedo bombers—and possibly some from Japanese midget subs that snuck into the harbor hours earlier—before capsizing in the shallow waters.

Trapped within the hull were more than four hundred officers and sailors. Rescue crews responded to the desperate pounding of survivors on the ship's steel plates with acetylene torches, sledgehammers, and pry bars to open a few holes and allow thirty-two of the crew to emerge and see sunlight once more. The remains of the rest laid mostly undisturbed until the Navy righted the ship in a Herculean salvage effort that took two-and-a-half years to complete. During the operation, Navy divers recovered some bodies as they cut away the super-structure of the upside-down battleship. Recovery of the vast majority of remains had to wait until hardpoints were welded onto the hull and scores of winches slowly wound thick steel cables to bring the vessel upright.

The remains, most of which were considered unidentifiable, were interred in a series of mass graves, but since the beginning of the twenty-first century advances in DNA technology have allowed the Defense POW/MIA Accounting Agency (DPAA) to send press releases and stories like this one from March 8, 2019:

DPAA identified U. S. Navy Fireman 1st Class Billy James Johnson on Feb. 26, 2019, marking him as the 200th crewman to be identified from the estimated 388 individual sets of remains that were designated as unknowns from the USS Oklahoma.

The story of identifying the remains and returning them to their families for proper burial took many twists and turns over nearly eight decades. The effort to finish the job could take decades longer, if it can ever realistically be accomplished.

The first Americans killed in the war are among the most recent to be identified.

The first complication was the state of the remains. The physical trauma caused by the torpedo explosions, decomposition of remains exposed to seawater and diesel fuel for more than two-and-half years, lack of technology available to medical examiners for making positive identifications, and the handling of the remains in the years immediately after they were recovered all made the task more difficult.

Two-and-a-half years after the USS *Oklahoma* capsized in Pearl Harbor, the battleship was righted, and four hundred remains were recovered. As of 2019 the Department of Defense POW/MIA Accounting Agency had identified half of the sailors.

Four hundred and fifteen Navy personnel and fourteen Marines were believed to have died in the sinking of *Oklahoma*, according to a 2010 memo written for DPAA by historian Heather Harris. Thirty-six were identified and buried in the next few years, leaving 393 sets of unidentified remains. In the difficult task of coming up with the most exact numbers possible, Harris notes the "discrepancies in the various casualty lists created after the attack on Pearl Harbor," and the further complication of sixty-four "unkowns" being recovered from the harbor waters, some of which could have been from *Oklahoma*.

Approximately four hundred sets of remains recovered from *Oklahoma* were interred in fifty-two common graves in the Nuuanu Cemetery or Halawa Naval Cemetery, according to Harris. There they remained until September 1947 when they were disinterred by the American Graves Registration Service and taken to Schofield Barracks Central Identification Laboratory. Harris noted "some confusion" in the records as to the condition of the remains when they were disinterred. While commingled remains had mostly likely been buried in groups shortly after recovery, they arrived at the laboratory in caskets "consisting of bones of a kind"—caskets filled only with skulls, or pelvic bones, or femurs and so forth.

Harris wrote that photographs of the processing of remains were later found showing laboratory staff cleaning commingled remains that arrived "in a highly jumbled state," still covered in diesel oil. Lab staff apparently cleaned the remains and grouped like remains together for identification processing.

In the case of skeletal remains, 1940s forensic identification relied largely on dental records and X-rays. For some enlisted men of the era, their first visit to a dentist might have come after they signed up. Grouping the skulls together for examination might have seemed the sensible method at the time.

Some confusion also arose as to how groups of remains should have been treated. Mass grave and group burial do not necessarily mean the same thing. While individuals' remains could not be identified, the U.S. Army Technical Manual expected that the names of the people within that group of unidentifiable remains would be. The examples Harris cites are when the victims of an airplane crash or a tank crew are known, but their remains have been rendered unidentifiable.

The Office of the Quartermaster General ordered that the segregation of remains by putting like parts into caskets was to cease and that efforts would be made to put together skeletal remains for possible identification. This raised a new concern about mixing up one man's remains with the remains of one or more other men, a forensic jigsaw puzzle of unbelievable complexity. The Quartermaster General ruled that even if a skull could be identified, "the American Graves Registration Service can not [sic], in good conscience, deliver the skull to the next of kin, or bury it in a government cemetery, as the only recoverable remains of a person."

The four hundred remains were reinterred in 1950 in the Nuuanu Memorial Cemetery Park "in sixty-one caskets interred in forty-five locations," Harris wrote.

Ray Emory was a survivor of Pearl Harbor and a researcher into the unknown remains from the attack. He found

documents from 1949 detailing a disagreement over the identification of partial remains believed to be those of Ensign
Eldon P. Wyman. The casket believed to contain Wyman's
remains were disinterred in 2003, leading to the official identification of his partial remains and those of several other men
with whom he was buried, Harris wrote.

"Subsequent anthropological, dental, and mtDNA (mito-
chondrial DNA) analysis of the remains in this casket have
revealed the presence of sparse remains of more than one hundred individuals," Harris wrote, revealing the complexity of
the task. That prompted the Navy and Marines to begin seeking out maternal relatives of *Oklahoma* crew members to cre-
ate a database that might one day lead to all the unidentified
getting their names restored to them.

That database now includes DNA samples for approximately 85 percent of the battleship's missing personnel. The
phased disinterment of the other sixty-one caskets began in
2015, according to DPAA.

One note about *Oklahoma:* Once it was righted, the Navy
determined the ship too damaged to return to service. After
the war it was decided to tow the ship to the mainland and
sell it for scrap. *Oklahoma* escaped that indignity, slipping
beneath the waves after its towline parted in heavy seas in May
1947.

Bibliography

Chapter One
"Army Battle Casualties and Nonbattle Deaths in World War II." Ibiblio website, n.d. http://www.ibiblio.org/hyperwar/USA/ref/Casualties/Casualties-1.html.

Encyclopaedia Britannica Online. "Bombing of Dresden: World War II," last modified February 6, 2020. https://www.britannica.com/event/bombing-of-Dresden.

"Penicillin," Medical Discoveries website, n.d. http://www.discoveriesinmedicine.com/Ni-Ra/Penicillin.html.

Simha, Rakesh Krishnan. "How India Bailed Out The West In World War II." *Swarajya Magazine*, May 24, 2015. https://

swarajyamag.com/magazine/how-india-bailed-out-the-west-in-world-war-ii.

Trueman, C N. "Medicine and Word War Two." The History Learning Site, March 6, 2015; last modified December 18, 2019. https://www.historylearningsite.co.uk/world-war-two/medicine-and-world-war-two/.

"U.S. Marine Corps Casualties From 1775 to the Present." United States Marines Virtual Birthplace Memorial website, n.d. http://www.usmarinesbirthplace.com/US-Marine-Corps-Casualties.html.

"World War II Casualties." Naval History and Heritage Command website, August 23, 2017. https://www.history.navy.mil/research/library/online-reading-room/title-list-alphabetically/w/world-war-ii-casualties.html.

"WWII Veterans Statistics: The Passing of the WWII Generation." National WWII Museum website, n.d. https://www.nationalww2museum.org/war/wwii-veteran-statistics.

Chapter Two
"Brief Overview of the Medical Department," WW2 US Medical Research Centre website, n.d. https://www.med-dept.com/articles/brief-overview-of-the-medical-department.

Hanley, Dick. "Hollywood to New Guinea," *Yank*, Old Magazine Articles website, July 21, 1944. http://www.oldmagazinearticles.com/Lew_Ayres_WW2_conscientious_objector.

"Penicillin," Medical Discoveries website, n.d. http://www.discoveriesinmedicine.com/Ni-Ra/Penicillin.html.

Trueman, C. N. "Medicine and Word War Two." The History Learning Site, March 6, 2015; last modified December 18, 2019. https://www.historylearningsite.co.uk/world-war-two/medicine-and-world-war-two/.

Vallance, Tom. "Obituary: Lew Ayres." *The Independent*, January 1, 1997, https://www.independent.co.uk/news/obituaries/obituary-lew-ayres-1281178.html.

Chapter Three
Bernstein, Adam. "Russell Johnson, Actor Who Played the Professor on Gilligan's Island,' dies at 89." *The Washington Post*, January 16, 2014.

Clark, Mike, and Rob Edelman. *Leonard Maltin's 2008 Movie Guide*. Edited by Leonard Maltin, Cathleen Anderson, and Luke Sader. New York: Signet Books, 2007.

Elhassan, Khalid. "From the Battlefield to Fame and Celebrity: 12 Famous World War II Veterans." History Collection website, October 5, 2017. https://historycollection.co/famous-wwii-veterans/.

Hevesi, Dennis. "Lee Marvin, Movie Tough Guy, Dies." *New York Times*, Aug. 31, 1987, A17.

Chapter Four
Bishop, Edward. *Mosquito: Wooden Wonder*. New York: Ballantine Books, 1971.

Hastings, Max. *Bomber Command: The Myths and Reality of the Strategic Bombing Offensive 1939-45*. New York: Dial Press/ James Wade, 1979.

"Interview with Bob Hoover at the National Museum of the USAF April 2014." YouTube, December 14, 2018. Video, 42:44. https://www.youtube.com/watch?v=o056xM04ltk.

Keeson, Arvid. "At Rest Far From Home: German Prisoners of War Were Killed after Germany Surrendered." Utah Stories website, May 24, 2018. https://utahstories.com/2018/05/ at-rest-far-from-home-german-war-dead-at-fort-douglas- were-killed-after-germany-surrendered/.

Mellow, Craig H. "Bob Hoover, Aviator Whose Aerobatic Stunts Are Legend, Dies at 94." *New York Times*, October 25, 2016, A29. https://www.nytimes.com/2016/10/26/us/bob-hoover-dead .html.

Scheong [psued.]. "Vaulting to Victory: The Story of the Wooden Horse." *Throughout History* (blog), April 12, 2011. https://www.throughouthistory.com/?p=1246.

"Shot Down Over France, 1944." Eyewitness to History, 1998. http://www.eyewitnesstohistory.com/shot.htm.

Stone, Eileen Hallet. "Living History: 'Midnight Massacre' in Utah Was Worst Mass Murder at a POW Camp in U.S. History." *Salt Lake Tribune*, Nov. 7, 2016. https://archive. sltrib.com/article.php?id=4546844&itype=CMSID.

Tanner, Todd, and Rebecca Green. "Uniquely Utah: New Museum Will Preserve Story of German POW Massacre in Salina." Fox 13 Salt Lake City, October 23, 2016. https:// fox13now.com/2016/10/23/uniquely-utah-new-museum-will-preserve-story-of-german-pow-massacre-in-salina/.

Winston, George. "World War Two Prisoner Of War Survivor Recalls the Wooden Horse." War History Online, November 29, 2015. https://www.warhistoryonline.com/war-articles/ world-war-two-survivor-recalls-great-escape.html.

Yeager, Chuck, and Leo Janos. *Yeager: An Autobiography*. New York: Random House, 1986.

Chapter Five

Cook, Tom, and Ian Duncan, dirs. *Nova*. Season 41, episode 12, "Escape from Nazi Alcatraz." Aired May 14, 2014, on PBS. https://www.tvguide.com/tvshows/nova/ episode-12-season-41/escape-from-nazi-alcatraz/191695/.

Joseph, Claudia. "Escape from Colditz— In a Glider Made with Sheets and Porridge: How One of the Most Audacious Escape

Plots Was Recreated." *Daily Mail*, August 4, 2012. https://www.dailymail.co.uk/news/article-2183626/Escape-Colditz--glider-sheets-porridge.html.

"The Flight From Colditz Finally Takes Off . . . 67 Years Later." RadioTimes website, August 13, 2012. https://www.radiotimes.com/news/2012-08-13/the-flight-from-colditz-finally-takes-off-67-years-later/.

Chapter Six
Barry, Tom. "Young MacArthur: A Different Drummer." Japan Brats Essays website, March 18, 2005. https://japanbratsessays.blogspot.com/2005/03/young-macarthur-different-drummer.html.

Craig, Olga. "Revealed: How Stalin's Brutal Massacre at Katyn Shamed his PoW Son Into Suicide." *Telegraph*. July 30, 2000. https://www.telegraph.co.uk/news/worldnews/europe/1351020/Revealed-how-Stalins-brutal-massacre-at-Katyn-shamed-his-PoW-son-into-suicide.html.

Frauenfelder, Mark. „'Why I Hate My Uncle' by William Hitler (*Look* magazine, 1939)." Boingboing website, April 28, 2017. https://boingboing.net/2017/04/28/why-i-hate-my-uncle-by-wi.html.

Godbey, Holly. "Stalin's Son Yakov Dzhugashvili Captured by the Germans. He 'Died' in a PoW Camp." War History Online, July 30, 2018. https://www.warhistoryonline.com/

world-war-ii/stalins-son-yakov-dzhugashvili-captured-by-the-germans-he-died-in-a-powcamp.html.

Martin, Douglas. "Lana Peters, Stalin's Daughter, Dies at 85." *New York Times*, November 28, 2011. A1. https://www.nytimes .com/2011/11/29/world/europe/stalins-daughter-dies-at-85 .html.

Milos, Knjaz. "Yakov and Vasily Stalin—Biography of Stalin's Sons." Foreign Policy website, May 9, 2018. https://foreignpolicyi. org/biography-of-stalins-sons-yakov-and-vasily-stalin/.

Phillips, Jack. "A Cursed Legacy: The Sad Lives of Stalin's Children." The Epoch Times website, March 8, 2017, last modified June 4, 2018. https://www.theepochtimes.com/a-cursed-legacy-the-sad-lives-of-stalins-children_2230736. html.

Phillips, John. "Romano Musolini: Jazz-Musician Son of 'Il Duce.'" *Independent*, February 4, 2006. https://www. independent.co.uk/news/obituaries/romano-mussolini-6109873.html.

Russell, Shahan. "William Hitler, Nephew of Adolf, Joined the US Navy to Fight the Nazis in WW2." War History Online, December 4, 2017. https://www.warhistoryonline. com/world-war-ii/william-hitler-didnt-join-the-nazis.html.

Scheong [pseud.]. "Vaulting to Victory: The Story of the Wooden Horse." *Throughout History* (blog), April 12, 2011. https://www.throughouthistory.com/?p=1246.

Shackle, Jerry. "Where Is Arthur MacArthur?" BDB website, n.d. http://www.bdb.co.za/shackle/articles/macarthur.htm.

Zimmerman, Dwight Jon. "The Tragedy of Yakov Stalin." Defense Media Network website, July 8, 2011. https://www. defensemedianetwork.com/stories/the-tragedy-of-yakov-stalin/.

Chapter Seven
Drury, Ian. "The Amazing Story of Mad Jack, the Hero Who Took on the Nazis with a Bow and Arrow (and Later Became a Professional Bagpipe Player)." *Daily Mail,* December 31, 2012, last modified January 1, 2013. https://www.dailymail. co.uk/news/article-2255533/The-amazing-story-Mad-Jack-hero-took-Nazis-bow-arrow-later-professional-bagpipe-player.html.

Forsyth, Rob. "The Churchill Brothers—Pre-War & WWII." Deddington   History.   http://www.deddingtonhistory.uk/worldwars/aparishatwar-postpublicationinformation/coloneljackandmajorgeneraltomchurchill.

Hough, Richard. *Mountbatten: A Biography.* New York: Random House, 1981.

Keegan, John, ed. *The Rand McNally Encyclopedia of World War II.* Greenwich, CT: Bison Books, 1977.

"Lieutenant-Colonel Jack Churchill." *Telegraph*, March 13, 1996. https://www.telegraph.co.uk/news/obituaries/7733516/Lieutenant-Colonel-Jack-Churchill.html.

Mason, David. *Raid on St. Nazaire*. New York: Ballantine Books, 1970.

Serena, Katie. "Mad Jack Churchill: World War II's Bagpipe Playing and Sword Wielding Badass." All That's Interesting, Nov. 21, 2007, last modified June 7, 2019. https://allthatsinteresting.com/mad-jack-churchill.

"Translated extract from a German Document on Their Capture." Commando Veterans Archive website, fig. http://gallery.commandoveterans.org/cdoGallery/v/WW2/Operation+Checkmate/Extract_from_Capture_Letter_P1_1_.jpg.html?g2_imageViewsIndex=1.

Walsh, Raoul, dir. *The Thief of Bagdad*. 1924.

Young, Peter. *Commando*. New York: Ballantine Books, 1969.

Chapter Eight
Associated Press. "Jackie Coogan Now Air Force Officer." *Free Lance-Star*, January 19, 1943. https://news.google.com/newspapers?id=4nNhAAAAIBAJ&sjid=0ooDAAAAIBAJ&pg=4971%2C5695150.

Barron, James. "Jackie Coogan, Child Star of Films, Dies at 69." *New York Times*, March 2, 1984. https://www.nytimes.com/1984/03/02/obituaries/jackie-coogan-child-star-of-films-dies-at-69.html.

"Freddie Once Had a Million." *Mail* (Adelaide), November 20, 1948. https://trove.nla.gov.au/newspaper/article/55899915.

United Press International. "Freddie Bartholomew Returned to Civilian Life: Injured in Service." *Warsaw Daily Union*, January 14, 1944. https://news.google.com/newspapers?id=BExfAAAAIBAJ&sjid=uVQNAAAAIBAJ&pg=2926,643298&dq=freddie+bartholomew&hl=en.

United Press International. "Jackie Coogan: Air Commando." *Sunday Morning Star*, March 19, 1943. https://news.google.com/newspapers.

Chapter Nine

Barbour, Alan G. *Humphrey Bogart*. New York: Pyramid Communications, 1973.

Hoyt, Edwin P. *McCampbell's Heroes: The Story of the U.S. Navy's Most Celebrated Carrier Fighter of the Pacific*. New York: Van Nostrand Reinhold, 1983.

MacIntyre, Donald. *Aircraft Carrier: The Majestic Weapon*. New York: Ballantine Books, 1968.

"Wayne Morris Succumbs at 45; Born in Padadena." *Pasadena Independent,* September 15, 1959. https://www.newspapers.com/clip/5840403/pasadena_independent/.

Chapter Ten
Berg, A. Scott. *Lindbergh.* New York: G. P. Putnam's Sons, 1998.

"Charles Lindbergh in Combat, 1944." Eyewitness to History, 2006.

Keegan, John, ed. *The Rand McNally Encyclopedia of World War II.* Greenwich, CT: Bison Books, 1977.

Whitman, Alden. "Lindbergh Says U.S. 'Lost' World War II." *New York Times,* Aug. 30, 1970. https://www.nytimes.com/1970/08/30/archives/lindbergh-says-us-lost-world-war-ii-lindbergh-contending-that-he.html.

Chapter Eleven
Ascheid, Antje. *Hitler's Heroines: Stardom and Womanhood in Nazi Cinema.* Philadelphia, PA: Temple University Press, 2003.

Clark, Mike, and Rob Edelman. *Leonard Maltin's 2008 Movie Guide.* Edited by Leonard Maltin, Cathleen Anderson, and Luke Sader. New York: A Plume Book. 2007.

Karpel, Dalia. "The Real Stanley Kubrick." Haarets website, November 3, 2005. https://www.haaretz.com/1.4880226.

Chapter Twelve

"Grodon Cummins." Murder in the UK. http://www. murderuk.com/serial_gordon_frederick_cummins.html.

Jenkins, John Philip. "Bruno Lüdke." Encyclopedia Britannica website, January 1, 2020. https://www.britannica.com/ biography/Bruno-Ludke.

Lane, Brian and Wilfred Gregg. *The Encyclopedia of Serial Killers*. London: Headline Book Publishing, 1992.

"Leonski, Enigma in Life and in Death, Carries His Secret to Grave." *Truth* (Sydney), November 15, 1942. http://trove.nla. gov.au/newspaper/article/168972547.

"Leonski Guilty on All Charges." *Age* (Melbourne), July 18, 1942. https://trove.nla.gov.au/newspaper/article/206813770.

Chapter Thirteen

Budanovic, Nikola. "The Day Japan Lost Her Airforce." War History Online, March 20, 2018. https://www.warhistoryonline. com/world-war-ii/the-day-japan-lost-her-airforce.html.

Hathaway, Henry, dir. *Wing and a Prayer.* 1944; Los Angeles: 20th Century Fox.

MacIntyre, Donald. *Aircraft Carrier: The Majestic Weapon.* New York: Ballantine Books, 1968.

Nevala-Lee, Alec. "On a Wing and a Prayer." *Alec Nevala-Lee* (blog). https://nevalalee.wordpress.com/2017/05/02/on-a-wing-and-a-prayer/.

Rooney, Andy. *My War.* New York: Crown Publishers, 1995.

Chapter Fourteen
Carter, Elliot. "How a Toilet Sunk a Deadly Nazi Submarine." *The National Interest,* March 9, 2019. https://nationalinterest.org/blog/buzz/how-toilet-sunk-deadly-nazi-submarine-46562.

"List of all U-Boats: U-1206." Uboat.net, n.d. https://uboat.net/boats/u1206.htm.

Mason, David. *U-Boat: The Secret Menace.* New York: Ballantine Books, 1968.

U.S. Navy. *The Fleet Type Submarine.* Chap. 9, "Water System." San Francisco Maritime National Park Association, 1946. https://maritime.org/doc/fleetsub/chap9.htm.

Chapter Fifteen
Kershaw, Alex. *Escape from The Deep: The Epic Story of a Legendary Submarine and Her Courageous Crew.* Boston: Da Capo Press, 2008.

"Tang (SS 306)." Naval History and Heritage Command website. https://www.history.navy.mil/content/history/nhhc/research/library/online-reading-room/title-list-alphabetically/u/united-states-submarine-losses/tang-ss-306.html.

Chapter Sixteen
Babb, Dave. "History of the Mule." American Mule Museum website. https://www.mulemuseum.org/history-of-the-mule.html.

Patowary, Kaushik. "Wojtek: The Bear That Drank Beer and Went to War." Amusing Planet, February 2018. https://www.amusingplanet.com/2018/02/wojtek-bear-that-drank-beer-and-went-to.html.

"Smarter than the Average Bear . . . By Far." *The Scotsman*, March 28, 2007. https://www.scotsman.com/lifestyle-2-15039/smarter-than-the-average-bear-by-far-1-1342563.

Waller, Anna M. *Horses and Mules and National Defense.* Washington, DC: Office of the Quartermaster General, 1958.

"Wojtek, the Bear That Fought in World War 2." Argunners Magazine website, April 10, 2018. https://www.argunners.com/wojtek-the-bear-that-fought-in-world-war-2/

Chapter Seventeen

Barker, A. J. *Suicide Weapon.* New York: Ballantine Books, 1971.

"Bolton Paul Defiant—British Fighter Plane." World War 2 Headquarters website, 2015. http://worldwar2headquarters. com/HTML/aircraft/britishAircraft/defiant.html.

Ford, Brian. *German Secret Weapons: Blueprint for Mars.* New York: Ballantine Books, 1969.

Green, William. *Rocket Fighter.* New York: Ballantine Books, 1971.

Keegan, John, ed. *The Rand McNally Encyclopedia of World War II.* Greenwich, CT: Bison Books, 1977.

Nesmith, Jeff. *No Higher Honor.* Marietta, GA: Longstreet, 1999.

Phaneuf, Brett. "D-Day—The Untold Story." BBC website, February 17, 2011. http://www.bbc.co.uk/history/ancient/ archaeology/marine_dday_underwater_01.shtml.

Chapter Eighteen

Harris, Heather. "History of the Sinking of USS *Oklahoma* and Subsequent Attempts to Recover and Identify Her Crew." Memorandum. Defense Prisoner of War Missing Personnel Office, April 10, 2012. https://www.public.navy. mil/bupers-npc/support/casualty/Documents/POW%20 MIA/USS%20OKLAHOMA%20(BB-37).pdf.

DPAA Public Affairs. "DPAA Makes 200th Identification from USS Oklahoma Unknown Remains." Defense POW/MIA Accounting Agency, March 8, 2019. https://www.dpaa.mil/News-Stories/Recent-News-Stories/Article/1779664/dpaa-makes-200th-identification-from-uss-oklahoma-unknown-remains/.

Hartshorn, Byron. "Salvaging the USS Oklahoma BB-37 at Pearl Harbor." *Byron Hartshorn* (blog), November 13, 2014. http://www.byronhartshorn.com/2014/11/13/salvaging-the-uss-oklahoma-bb-37-at-pearl-harbor/.

"Salvage of USS Oklahoma , 1942–1944." Naval History and Heritage Command website, n.d. https://www.history.navy.mil/content/history/nhhc/our-collections/photography/wars-and-events/world-war-ii/pearl-harbor-raid/post-attack-ship-salvage/salvage-of-uss-oklahoma--1942-1944.html.

Maddux, Vernon. "Did A Japanese Midget Submarine Sink the USS Oklahoma on December 7, 1941?" *Western Americana: History of the American West,* April 11, 2010. https://westernamericana2.blogspot.com/2010/04/did-japanese-midget-submarine-sink-uss.html.

Acknowledgments

After writing, rewriting, and staring at a page for a few hours, the author might believe that what he or she wrote makes perfect sense. That is when the writer is in most need of an editor. I had two—Julie Ganz and Johanna Fortescue at Skyhorse Publishing—who took what I had written and cleared up a number of issues, along with addressing matters of formatting and style. Coming from a background in newspapers, anything over twenty column inches seems like an epic. For their assistance, I am deeply grateful.

To my wife, Jennie, and daughters, Megan and Laura, I owe my thanks for their patience, support, technical assistance, and some very good ideas about stories to include in this book.